PORTLAND TRAVEL GUIDE 2023

Explore Portland: Comprehensive guide to
when to visit, what to do and places to visit

Diana H. Cayer

TABLE OF CONTENT

INTRODUCTION..7

   History of Portland 9

   Geography and climate................................13

   Why visit Portland? 16

CHAPTER 1 20

   Planning your trip...20

   Best Time to Visit...22

   Portland's transportation 25

   Public transit 25

   Bicycling..26

   Driving...27

   A day trip...28

   Tips for travelers 28

   What to bring 32

CHAPTER 2 35

   Getting to Portland......................................35

   By air...37

   By train..39

   By car..42

   By bus...45

CHAPTER 3 48

   Accommodation options in Portland.............48

   Hotels..50

   Motels 53

   Bed and breakfasts.....................................55

   Hostels..58

Vacation Rentals 60

Boutique Inns 63

CHAPTER 4 66

Top Portland Attractions 66

Portland Museum of Art 67

Pittock House 71

Portland Zoo 73

Japanese Garden in Portland 77

City of Books Powell 81

Park Washington 84

Lan Su Chinese Garden 87

Garden of International Rose Tests 91

CHAPTER 5 95

Portland Outdoor Activities 95

Trails for biking and hiking 97

Forest Park 100

Park at Tom McCall Waterfront 102

Portland Saturday market 105

Wine Tasting 108

CHAPTER 6 112

Neighborhoods in Portland 112

Portland's downtown 115

The Background of Portland's Downtown 115

District of Pearl 117

History of Pearl District 117

Living in the Pearl District 118

Dining and shopping in the Pearl District 119

Cultural Activities in the Pearl District 120

Alberta Arts District 121

Mississippi Avenue 125

Hawthorne neighborhood.. 129

Division Street Neighborhood 132

CHAPTER 7 136

Portland day trips.. 136

Falls Multnomah.. 137

Columbia River Gorge 138

Mount Hood 142

Willamette Valley Wine Country.. 145

CHAPTER 8 148

Portland's Restaurants and Bars 148

Portland's Restaurant Scene 149

Cafes and coffee shops 152

Distilleries and Breweries.. 155

Pods and carts for food.. 158

Farmers' markets 162

CHAPTER 9 166

Practical Information 166

Safety and health 168

Emergency Information... 170

Sustainable Travel Advice 173

Exchange of money and currencies...................................... 177

Currencies accepted in Portland... 177

Portland's exchange rates for currency.................................. 178

Money Exchange Options in Portland.................................... 179

Language.. 181

Spoken Languages in Portland.. 181

Language and the Identity of Portland 183

Useful Phrases 184

Local customs and etiquette 187

CONCLUSION 191

Recommendation... 194

INTRODUCTION

W elcome to Portland, Oregon, sometimes known as the Rose City! Portland, a thriving and culturally diverse city in the Pacific Northwest of the United States, has something to offer everyone. Portland has become a well-liked travel destination for travelers from all over the world thanks to its breathtaking natural landscape, renowned food and drink scene, and progressive, eccentric culture.

Portland is a city that takes pride in its dedication to local businesses, sustainability, and creativity. Portland is a terrific city to explore by foot, bike, or public transportation because of its bike-friendly streets, robust public transportation system, and walkable neighborhoods. The city's numerous parks and green areas are available for visitors to enjoy, including Forest Park, the biggest urban park in the United States, and the International Rose Test Garden, which has over 10,000 roses.

Portland is renowned for having some of the world's top coffee shops, microbreweries, and food carts in its food and beverage industry. Visitors can choose from a wide variety of cuisines and flavors to suit their tastes, from the award-winning restaurants of downtown to the food carts of Southeast Portland.

Portland has a flourishing arts and music scene in addition to its natural beauty and cuisine culture. The Portland Art Museum, the Oregon Historical Society, and the Museum of Contemporary Craft are just a few of the city's many museums and galleries. From small jazz bars to huge concert halls, music enthusiasts can enjoy a variety of live music venues.

Whether you enjoy the outdoors, good food, or the arts, Portland has something to offer. Come experience everything that the Rose City has to offer by traveling there!

History of Portland

The largest city in the state of Oregon is Portland, which is situated in the Pacific Northwest of the country. Over the course of its long history, which spans more than 10,000 years, the city has hosted numerous indigenous tribes as well as explorers and settlers from Europe. This essay will examine Portland's history from its earliest days to the present.

The Chinook, Clackamas, and Tualatin tribes, who lived along the Columbia and Willamette rivers, were the first people to live in the Portland area. These tribes were expert hunters and fisherman, and they established a sophisticated trading system that covered the entire area. This way of life was disrupted in the 18th century by European explorers who brought new diseases and took over the land.

The first European to cross the Columbia River was Captain Robert Gray in 1792, and the Lewis and Clark expedition arrived in the region in 1805. In the 1820s, the Hudson's Bay Company erected a fur-trading post at Fort Vancouver, directly across the river from Portland, as a result of these voyages, which allowed for further exploration and settlement of the area.

William Overton and Asa Lovejoy led a group of immigrants who arrived in the region in 1843 and built a tiny settlement on the Willamette River's west bank. The town was given the name Portland after Overton's business partner, whose hometown was Portland, Maine. After the city was formally incorporated in 1851, it grew quickly.

Due to its location at the meeting point of the Columbia and Willamette rivers, Portland developed into a significant shipping and transportation hub throughout the middle of the 19th century. The city swiftly developed into a hub for the logging and fishing industries due to its strategic location as a port for products going to and from Asia and Europe.

Early in the 20th century, Portland saw a period of significant urbanization and growth. The population of the city increased as more immigrants from Europe and Asia arrived, and it developed into a major hub for manufacturing, trade, and banking. Portland held the Lewis and Clark Centennial Exposition in 1905, which attracted over 1.5 million visitors and contributed to Portland's development as a significant cultural hub.

In the 20th century, Portland kept expanding and changing. The city experienced a significant urban renewal initiative in the 1950s and 1960s, which led to the construction of numerous new structures and public areas. Portland rose to prominence in the 1970s and 1980s as a result of its progressive politics and environmental activism, serving as a role model for sustainable urban growth.

Today, Portland is a thriving, multicultural city with a population of over 600,000. It is renowned for its thriving food and beverage business, vibrant arts and cultural scene, and dedication to sustainability and environmentalism. Even though the city has recently dealt with issues like homelessness, housing affordability, and racial inequality, it still manages to draw in new residents and tourists from all over the world.

The history of Portland is an intriguing and intricate tale that represents the numerous individuals and cultures that have called this city home. Portland has undergone many changes over the years, from its beginnings as a trading station to its current status as a significant metropolitan area, but it has always remained a hub of invention, creativity, and resiliency. The city will definitely encounter new difficulties and opportunities as it develops, but its vibrant character and rich history will always be at the core of who it is.

Geography and climate

T he city of Portland is found in the state of Oregon, in the Pacific Northwest region of the United States. It has a special topography and climate that contribute to its distinctive character, and it is renowned for its natural beauty. The location, topography, and weather patterns of Portland, as well as its geography and climate, will all be covered in this essay.

Geography

The Willamette Valley, which extends from Eugene in the south to Portland in the north, is where Portland is located. The Coast Range, the Cascade Range, and the Columbia River Gorge are all mountain ranges that encircle the valley on all sides. The city's distinctive terrain is influenced by these natural elements, which include hills, valleys, and rivers that produce a varied and dynamic environment.

Portland is divided into the west side and the east side by the Willamette River, which also passes through the center of the city. The city's downtown, as well as many of its historic neighborhoods and cultural institutions, are located on the west side. With its varied neighborhoods, hip eateries, and vibrant arts scene, the east side is renowned for its more relaxed atmosphere.

Climate

Portland has a temperate oceanic climate, which is distinguished by mild annual average temperatures and moderate annual precipitation. The city's proximity to the Pacific Ocean and the Columbia River Gorge has an impact on the region's weather patterns by bringing in cool ocean air and moisture.

Normal summertime temperatures in Portland range from the mid-60s to the mid-80s Fahrenheit (about 16 to 30 degrees Celsius), making for warm and pleasant conditions. Outdoor pursuits like hiking, biking, and kayaking are also popular at this period, as are cultural activities like music festivals and culinary fairs.

On the other hand, Portland's winters are frequently wet and frigid, with temperatures between the mid-30s and the mid-50s Fahrenheit (about 1 to 13 degrees Celsius). Snowfall is sporadic in the city, albeit it is uncommon and usually does not accumulate. Despite the rain, many residents make the most of the colder months by huddling in coffee shops, visiting art museums, or taking part in the city's numerous indoor activities.

The "June gloom," a period of chilly and cloudy weather that frequently happens in early summer, is one of the most unusual meteorological occurrences in Portland. With cloudy sky and temperatures that are colder than usual for the time of year, this can linger for several weeks. Despite the cloudy skies, many Portlanders value the chance to relax and take in the cooler weather before the summer heat arrives.

Portland's topography and climate have a big impact on the way of life and character of the city. Portland has a variety of outdoor activities and beautiful scenery because of its closeness to mountains, rivers, and the ocean. While the city's cloudy summers and rainy winters may not be to everyone's taste, they are an essential component of the city's charm and identity.

Why visit Portland?

Portland is a vibrant, distinctive city that provides tourists with a wide range of activities and attractions. Portland offers something for everyone, whether you want to experience the great outdoors, indulge in delicious food and beverages, or immerse yourself in the vibrant arts and culture scene. We'll go through a few of the factors encouraging you to visit Portland in this essay.

The Natural World

Portland's natural beauty and wealth of outdoor activities are two of its key draws. There are numerous options for hiking, biking, kayaking, and other outdoor activities because the city is surrounded by mountains, forests, and rivers. Within the city limits, visitors can stroll through the Japanese Garden, a tranquil haven of peace and beauty, or explore Forest Park, one of the biggest urban parks in the

United States. Visitors can also take a short trip to the breathtaking Columbia River Gorge or walk up Mount Hood, an active volcano that towers over the region.

Food and beverage

Portland has a booming culinary culture that highlights the best of Pacific Northwest cuisine, earning it the moniker "foodies' paradise." Numerous farm-to-table restaurants, craft breweries, and artisanal bakeries that use regional, sustainable ingredients are located throughout the city. There are plenty of delectable options to pick from, whether you're searching for a traditional brunch experience in Portland, a fine dining tasting menu, or a fun food cart experience.

A Culture

Portland boasts a vibrant and varied arts and cultural scene, with top-notch galleries, theaters, and museums that include everything from classical music to contemporary art. The Arlene Schnitzer Concert Hall, the Portland Art Museum, and the city's many independent book and record stores are all accessible to visitors. A number of festivals and events are also held in the city throughout the year, such as the PDX Jazz Festival, the Portland International Film Festival, and the Portland Rose Festival.

The Sustainability

With a culture that prioritizes eco-friendly living and sustainable activities, Portland is famous for its dedication to sustainability and environmentalism. The city has an extensive network of bike lanes and walkways that make it simple to explore the city without a car, as well as a public transportation system that includes buses, light rail, and streetcars.

Additionally, Portland is home to a sizable local food movement that supports modest-scale farmers and producers, as well as a large number of eco-friendly businesses and organizations.

The people

Portland is renowned for its hospitable locals who are enthusiastic about their city and willing to share it with tourists. Portlanders are happy to offer advice, share their stories, and make you feel at home in their city, whether you're speaking with a local at a coffee shop, perusing the goods at a craft market, or attending a community event.

In addition to its natural beauty and outdoor activities, Portland also has a thriving food and drink industry, arts and cultural scene, sustainability initiatives, and hospitable locals. Portland is a place that is certain to make an impact, whether you're planning a weekend visit or a longer stay.

CHAPTER 1

Planning your trip

It can be fun and gratifying to organize a trip to Portland, Oregon. Portland, known for its breathtaking natural beauty, top-notch cuisine, and thriving arts and culture scene, has something to offer every kind of traveler. Portland is a place you should not miss if you enjoy good food, the outdoors, history, or simply want a change of scenery.

Planning a trip to Portland can be difficult, though, because there is so much to see and do there. What hotel should you book? Which sights should you not miss? How can you utilize your time in the city to the fullest? We'll provide you all the details you need to make the ideal Portland travel arrangements in this guide.

We'll start by talking about the ideal season to visit Portland and what to anticipate in terms of the weather and crowds. We'll also discuss the city's various districts and what they have to offer, from the fashionable shops and eateries of the Pearl District to Southeast Portland's laid-back atmosphere.

We'll next delve into all of Portland's attractions and activities, including bicycling and hiking in Forest Park and discovering the city's famed food and drink scene. The Portland Art Museum, Powell's City of Books, and the Oregon Museum of Science and Industry are just a few of the cultural attractions and must-see sites we'll recommend.

We'll also provide directions and advice on using the public transportation system, renting bikes, and driving about Portland. We'll go through how to arrange day trips to surrounding locations like the Columbia River Gorge or Mount Hood as well as the best methods to navigate the city's numerous bridges, highways, and public transit lines.

Finally, we'll discuss useful facts like how to budget for your trip, where to find lodging in Portland, and what to bring for the weather in the Pacific Northwest. Additionally, we'll offer suggestions for the top cafes, bars, and eateries in the area, from popular craft breweries and distilleries to traditional brunch spots in Portland.

Whether you're a seasoned traveler or a first-time visitor to Portland, at the end of this book, you'll have all the resources you need to organize an enjoyable trip. So prepare to explore all that Portland has to offer by packing your luggage, grabbing your hiking boots, and getting started.

Best Time to Visit

Every season has something to offer in Portland, Oregon. It's no surprise that tourists swarm to Portland year-round given the city's moderate temperature and plenty of outdoor activities. The greatest time to visit Portland, however, primarily depends on what you want to do while there. In this essay, we'll discuss Portland's several seasons and highlight the ideal times to travel based on your interests.

Summer (June through August)

Portland experiences its busiest travel season in the summer, and for good reason. It's the ideal time of year to explore the city's many parks, gardens, and outdoor attractions because of the mild temperatures and clear skies. The number of festivals and events that take place during the summer in Portland is one of its main attractions. There is usually something going on in the city during the summer, from the Oregon Brewers Festival in July to the Portland Rose Festival in June.

Autumn (September to November)

Portland is especially lovely in the fall, especially if you enjoy viewing the changing leaves. The city's many parks and gardens become even more magnificent as the leaves begin to change hues. As many of the nearby wineries start their harvest season in September and October, these are also fantastic months to travel if you're interested in wine tasting.

December to February

Despite not being recognized for its snowy winters, Portland nevertheless has a ton of wintertime activities to offer tourists. There are plenty of festive things to do in Portland throughout the winter, from ice skating at the outdoor rink in Pioneer Courthouse Square to seeing a holiday performance at the Oregon Symphony. Additionally, if you enjoy winter sports, the nearby Mt. Hood ski areas are easily accessible.

March to May

Portland is especially lovely in the spring if you want to enjoy the many blooming and flowers that the city has to offer. There are many vibrant plants to appreciate in Portland during the spring, from the well-known cherry blossoms in the Japanese Garden to the breathtaking rhododendrons at the Crystal Springs Rhododendron Garden. Before the summer tourists arrive, spring is a terrific time to explore the city's various hiking trails and parks.

Overall, your interests and the things you want to accomplish during your vacation will determine when is the best time to visit Portland. Portland provides something for every season, whether you want to enjoy the sunshine in one of the city's numerous parks, discover its vibrant food and drink culture, or take in the splendor of the Pacific Northwest.

Portland's transportation

Visitors may easily travel the city and neighboring areas in Portland, Oregon because to the city's diverse and effective transportation options. Portland features a range of transportation alternatives, including bike-friendly streets and public transit options, making it a great travel destination.

Public transit

Public transportation is one of the most well-liked and economical ways to move about Portland. In the city and its surrounding suburbs, the TriMet system provides bus, light rail, and streetcar services. The streetcar is a practical method to travel around Portland's hip neighborhoods, while the MAX light rail system makes it simple to get to downtown.

The Portland Streetcar provides a free ride zone that includes numerous well-known sites for guests staying in the downtown area, making it simple and convenient to go about. Additionally, TriMet provides a mobile ticketing app that enables users to buy and use tickets on their smartphones, doing away with the need to carry cash or figure out how to use ticket machines.

Bicycling

With a wide network of bike lanes, bike parking, and bike-sharing programs, Portland is one of the most bicycle-friendly cities in the US. Visitors can either use the Biketown bike-sharing service, which offers short-term rentals of bright orange bikes stationed all throughout the city, or hire bikes from one of the many bike rental shops the city has to offer.

It's simple to get around on a bike in many of Portland's key districts and attractions, making it a fantastic way to see the city while getting some exercise. The Springwater Corridor Trail, a beautiful 21-mile bike path that connects downtown Portland to the suburbs, is available for those seeking a lengthier ride.

Driving

Driving in Portland is an alternative, however it should be noted that during rush hours, traffic can become backed up. Before renting a car, visitors may want to think about other modes of transportation since parking can be both expensive and difficult in the downtown area.

If visitors do decide to drive, it's crucial to be mindful of Portland's unusual street structure, which features a grid system in the city center and some diagonal streets that can be perplexing to people who aren't familiar with the area. Furthermore, some streets have dedicated bike lanes, so drivers need to be aware of them.

A day trip

There are numerous modes of transportation available for tourists who want to see the locations outside of Portland. Daily transportation is provided by the Columbia Gorge Express from Portland to Multnomah Falls, a well-liked natural landmark in the Columbia River Gorge. The Amtrak Cascades train, which travels between Portland and Seattle and other cities along the Pacific Northwest coast, is another option for tourists.

Every traveler's demands are met by Portland's convenient and numerous transportation alternatives. Portland provides a multitude of methods to get around and discover everything the city and surrounding areas have to offer, whether you decide to use the city's public transportation system, hire a bike, or travel by vehicle.

Tips for travelers

It might be thrilling to visit a new city, but it can also be intimidating to get around in a new location with strange cultures and ways of living. Portland, Oregon is a distinctive and exciting city with a lot to offer visitors, but in order to get the most of your vacation, it's crucial to be well-prepared. Here are a few recommendations for visitors to Portland:

The weather in Portland is infamous for being erratic, with rain and sunshine frequently occurring on the same day. If you intend to explore the outdoors, pack layers and waterproof apparel.

Accept Public Transportation: Portland boasts a dependable and effective bus, light rail, and streetcar system. Use these methods to save money and stay out of traffic.

Bring comfy shoes: Because Portland is a walkable city and many of its attractions can be reached on foot. Bring appropriate walking shoes if you intend to explore the city on foot.

Try the local Cuisine: Portland is renowned for its culinary scene, which places a focus on fresh, locally-sourced ingredients and creative preparations. Try new restaurants and cuisines without reservation, and don't forget to sample some of the city's well-known food carts.

Respect the Environment: Portland is a city that places a high priority on the environment and sustainability. Be considerate of the city's environment and think about bringing reusable bags, water bottles, and cutlery with you.

Explore the Outdoors: Portland is surrounded by stunning natural features like rivers, mountains, and forests. Take advantage of the city's outdoor activities, whether it's kayaking on the Willamette River or hiking in Forest Park.

Be Prepared for Crowds: Portland is a well-liked tourist destination, particularly in the summer. At popular attractions and eateries, be prepared for crowds and think about making reservations in advance.

Be Open-Minded: Portland is a diverse and inviting city known for its progressive principles and a vibrant LGBTQ+ community. While visiting, keep an open mind and show respect for other people's cultures and ways of life.

Visit the Neighborhoods: Portland is made up of a number of distinctive neighborhoods, each of which has a unique character and set of amenities. To get a flavor of the city's different neighborhoods, make sure to visit places like the Pearl District, Alberta Arts District, and Hawthorne Boulevard.

Take it Easy: Portland is a city that embraces leisure and a slower pace of life. Enjoy the coffee shops, parks, and outdoor areas of the city and soak up the relaxed atmosphere.

Travelers may maximize their time in Portland by using the advice in this article to take full advantage of everything that this distinctive and lively city has to offer.

What to bring

It's critical to pack appropriately for Portland, Oregon's distinct climate and culture while making travel plans. Consider packing the following essentials for your trip:

Waterproof Clothing: Portland is renowned for its wet climate, so bring an umbrella, rain boots, and a waterproof jacket. You can explore the city dry while doing this.

Layers: Are a good idea because Portland's summers may still be cold and damp. To stay comfortable all day, pack layers that are simple to add or remove.

Bring comfortable shoes: If you plan to explore Portland on foot as it is a walking city. If you intend to go hiking in the neighboring mountains or forests, you might want to bring hiking shoes.

Reusable Water Bottle: Because Portland is committed to sustainability and waste reduction, you might want to bring a reusable water bottle that you can fill up at one of the numerous water fountains and filling stations the city has.

Sun protection: Although Portland is renowned for its heavy rainfall, the city can also experience bright, sunny weather in the summer. For sun protection, don't forget to carry sunscreen, sunglasses, and a hat.

Local Beer and Wine: Since Portland has a thriving craft beer and wine sector, think about bringing a growler or wine carrier to bring some of the city's delectable libations home.

Camera: From the city's distinctive architecture to its vibrant street art, Portland is a lovely place with many photo opportunities.

Cash and Credit Cards: While credit cards are accepted almost everywhere in Portland, certain tiny shops and food carts could only take cash. Make sure to keep both in a variety.

Book or Guidebook: There are many excellent books and guides available to learn more about the city's distinctive features and attractions. Portland has a rich history and culture.

Comfortable Backpack or Tote Bag: When visiting the city, you'll need to carry all of your belongings in a comfortable, long-lasting backpack or tote bag.

Travelers can maximize their time in Portland by carrying these goods so that they are ready for the city's distinctive climate and culture.

CHAPTER 2

Getting to Portland

Portland, Oregon, a bustling and dynamic city with a natural beauty, progressive culture, and a booming food and drink scene, is situated in the Pacific Northwest of the United States. Getting to Portland is simple because to the city's convenient location and a variety of transportation choices, whether you're travelling for business or pleasure.

The primary airport serving the city is Portland International Airport (PDX), which is only 12 miles northeast of downtown Portland. Major airlines like Delta, American, United, and Alaska Airlines operate out of PDX and offer flights to and from locations all over the world.

Portland is conveniently reachable by vehicle via major routes including I-5 and I-84. I-5 takes three hours to travel south from Seattle, and ten hours to travel south from San

Francisco. I-84, which connects Portland to places like Boise and Salt Lake City, is accessible from the east.

Amtrak provides daily train service to Portland from Eugene and Los Angeles in the south and Seattle and Vancouver in the north for passengers arriving by train. Portland's Union Station is situated in the center of the city's downtown, making it simple to get to the area's numerous attractions and neighborhoods.

Buses, light rail, streetcars, and taxis are just a few of the alternatives for getting around Portland after you are there. With many streets that are bike-friendly and designated bike lanes, biking is also a common way to move about the city. Portland has a large number of walkable areas and parks for individuals who want to explore on foot.

Portland's central position and a variety of transit choices make getting there simple and convenient. The city offers a warm welcome and plenty of options for discovery and adventure, whether you're arriving by flight, car, train, or bus.

By air

With Portland International Airport (PDX) being only 12 miles northeast of downtown Portland, Portland, Oregon, is a thriving and dynamic city that is simple to reach by flight. The airport offers flights to and from locations all over the world and serves as a hub for major airlines like Delta, American, United, and Alaska Airlines.

There are many ways to get to and from the airport for those flying into Portland, including public transit, ride-sharing services, and rental automobiles.

To and from the airport, public transit is an economical and practical option. Direct service to the airport from downtown Portland is provided by the MAX light rail system, with trains leaving every 15 minutes during peak hours and every 30 minutes during off-peak hours. Depending on the time of day, tickets for the 40-minute travel from Portland's downtown to the airport range from $2.50 to $5.

The airport also offers ride-sharing services like Uber and Lyft, with specific pick-up and drop-off areas situated right outside of baggage claim. Prices vary based on the hour and distance traveled, but they might be a practical choice for people going together or with luggage.

Major businesses including Avis, Budget, Enterprise, and Hertz have rental cars available at the airport for people who want to have their own mode of transportation. The rental vehicle counters are situated on the lower level of the airport, and shuttle buses run to and from the rental car lot.

When you come to Portland, there are several of ways to move around the city, including streetcars, light rail, buses, and taxis. Many of the city's attractions, such as downtown Portland, the Pearl District, and the Oregon Convention Center, are easily accessible via the MAX light rail system. The cost of a taxi from the airport to downtown Portland is typically around $35.

With a variety of ways to get to and from the airport, traveling to and from Portland by plane is simple and practical. Portland welcomes you with open arms and provides a wealth of options for exploration and adventure, whether you're visiting for business or pleasure.

By train

The largest city in Oregon, Portland, is a stunning tourist attraction that draws people from all over the world. Although many people opt to drive or fly to Portland, taking the train can also be a pleasant and picturesque option. This essay will discuss the advantages of taking the train to Portland as well as some suggestions for maximizing your trip.

The breathtaking scenery you will see en route is one of the main benefits of taking the train to Portland. Portland is a stop on the Coast Starlight route of Amtrak, which runs from Los Angeles to Seattle. The train travels every day and the trip lasts about 35 hours.

The route passes through some of the most picturesque regions of the West Coast, including as the Columbia River

Gorge, the Cascade Mountains, and the Pacific Ocean coastline. As you travel down the tracks, you'll be treated to beautiful views of rocky cliffs, deep forests, and glittering waterfalls.

The ability to unwind and relish the journey is another advantage of taking the train. Unlike driving, when you must pay attention to the road and navigate through traffic, taking the train lets you relax and take in the views. You can read a book, watch a movie, or just sit and take in the sights from the window.

Additionally, Amtrak trains feature spacious seating, lots of legroom, and on-board conveniences like lounges and dining cars. You can choose a private sleeper cabin if you're flying overnight for more comfort and solitude.

There are various things you can do to make the most of your train ride to Portland. First, if you're going overnight, think about upgrading to a sleeper car. You'll have extra room to spread out and a personal area to unwind and sleep as a result. Additionally, you can benefit from the on-board dining car, which offers delectable dishes made with fresh, regional ingredients. Bring a camera to capture the breathtaking sights along the route, and wear layers of clothing because the weather might change frequently.

There are lots of things to see and do in Portland once you get there. The city is renowned for its thriving farm-to-table gastronomy, local brewers, and arts sector. Wander through the Pearl District, which features chic stores, galleries, and eateries housed in old structures.

Explore the Portland Art Museum or go to Powell's City of Books, the biggest independent bookstore in the world. Check out some of the city's well-known breweries, including Deschutes, BridgePort, and Rogue Ales, if you enjoy beer.

A distinctive and entertaining experience, taking the train to Portland will give you the chance to take in some of the most beautiful West Coast countryside. Taking the train is a great option for those looking to travel to Portland because it has comfortable seating, on-board amenities, and the chance to unwind and enjoy the journey. When you get there, you'll discover a bustling metropolis with many of activities to check out. Pack your luggage, board the train, and get set for a once-in-a-lifetime experience in Portland.

By car

Many visitors choose to drive to Portland, whether they are doing so from surrounding towns or starting a cross-country road trip. In this essay, we'll look at the advantages of driving to Portland and offer some advice on how to make the most of your trip.

Driving to Portland offers flexibility, which is one of its main benefits. You have the option to determine your route and make stops along the way when traveling by automobile. You can choose between a more direct route through the mountains or the scenic path by the seaside.

Along the trip, you can also make stops at sights and locations including Mount Hood and Crater Lake National

Park. Having a car in Portland also allows you to take your time discovering the city and its surroundings.

The chance to view the varied Pacific Northwest landscapes is another advantage of travelling to Portland. You'll come across breathtaking landscape as you travel through Oregon, including woods, mountains, and waterfalls.

Additionally, you'll travel through quaint towns and cities, each with its own distinct personality and attractions. Driving will give you the chance to take in the beauty and diversity of the area in a manner that flying would not allow you to.

There are various things you may do to maximize your driving time to Portland. Start by researching any must-see locations or attractions along the road as you arrange your trip. This will enable you to maximize your time and guarantee that you don't miss any exciting possibilities. Pack any required maps or navigational aids, as well as snacks and beverages for the journey. Additionally, be sure to be ready for any snow or ice conditions you may encounter if you're traveling in the winter.

There are lots of things to see and do in Portland once you get there. The city is renowned for its thriving farm-to-table gastronomy, local brewers, and arts sector. Wander through the Pearl District, which features chic stores, galleries, and eateries housed in old structures.

Explore the Portland Art Museum or go to Powell's City of Books, the biggest independent bookstore in the world. Check out some of the city's well-known breweries, including Deschutes, BridgePort, and Rogue Ales, if you enjoy beer.

If you want to see the diversity and splendor of the Pacific Northwest, driving to Portland is a fantastic alternative. Driving gives you the flexibility to select your own path and make any necessary pauses, which lets you design a singular and individualized travel experience. When you get to Portland, you'll discover a bustling city with lots of attractions to check out. Pack your luggage, get in the car, and prepare for a once-in-a-lifetime experience in Portland.

By bus

For many tourists, taking a bus to Portland is a practical and affordable choice. Several bus companies provide daily service from cities all over the region to Portland, making taking the bus an excellent way to see the Pacific Northwest. This post will discuss the advantages of taking the bus to Portland as well as some suggestions for maximizing your trip.

The cost-effectiveness of taking the bus to Portland is one of its main benefits. Bus travel is a viable choice for travelers on a tight budget because tickets are frequently significantly less expensive than those for trains or airplanes.

Additionally, a lot of bus companies give discounts to people in the military, senior citizens, and students. Bus travel is a great method to see the area without spending a fortune for individuals without access to a car.

The convenience of bus travel is another advantage. Bus companies usually offer a variety of daily departure times from large cities, making it simple to select one that fits into your schedule. In addition, a lot of bus operators include comforts like Wi-Fi, charging stations, and cozy seating to make the trip more enjoyable. Taking the bus also relieves the stress of dealing with traffic and parking, as the driver handles everything.

There are various things you can do to maximize your bus trip from Seattle to Portland. First, because many bus companies do not provide on-board refreshments, think about packing snacks and drinks for the journey. Bring whatever entertainment or reading materials you might need to pass the time during the travel. Dress in layers if you're traveling in the winter because the temperature on the bus can change.

There are lots of things to see and do in Portland once you get there. The city is renowned for its thriving farm-to-table gastronomy, local brewers, and arts sector. Wander through the Pearl District, which features chic stores, galleries, and eateries housed in old structures.

Explore the Portland Art Museum or go to Powell's City of Books, the biggest independent bookstore in the world. Check out some of the city's well-known breweries, including Deschutes, BridgePort, and Rogue Ales, if you enjoy beer.

For those who want to travel cheaply and conveniently through the Pacific Northwest, taking the bus to Portland is a good choice. Bus travel can be a relaxing and delightful experience because to the numerous daily departures and amenities like Wi-Fi and comfy seating. When you get to Portland, you'll discover a bustling city with lots of attractions to check out. Pack your luggage, board the bus, and get ready for a once-in-a-lifetime experience in Portland.

CHAPTER 3

Accommodation options in Portland

The city of Portland, Oregon, is well-known for its vivacious and diverse culture, breathtaking natural beauty, and dedication to sustainability and ecology. It thus became a well-liked tourism destination for visitors from all over the world. Additionally, Portland is home to a wide range of lodging options that meet the requirements and taste of various types of visitors.

Portland has accommodations to suit every taste, whether you're searching for a plush hotel with all the bells and whistles, a quaint bed & breakfast, or a cheap hostel. Each district in the city has its own distinct personality and allure, and this is mirrored in the kinds of accommodations that are offered there.

Some of Portland's most recognizable lodgings, including the venerable Benson Hotel and the opulent Nines Hotel, can be found downtown. These hotels have first-rate extras like fine dining restaurants, exercise centers, and rooftop bars with spectacular city views.

Consider staying in one of Portland's many unique and attractive bed and breakfasts if you want a more relaxed setting. These establishments provide visitors with a more individualized and intimate experience because they are frequently housed in historic structures.

Portland also features a large selection of hostels and low-cost hotels that provide economical lodging without compromising quality or convenience for individuals on a tight budget. These homes are frequently found in some of Portland's most lively and diverse communities, like the Hawthorne District and the Alberta Arts District.

Last but not least, Portland is renowned for its dedication to sustainability and ecology, which is reflected in the abundance of environmentally friendly and sustainable lodging options that can be found all throughout the city. These buildings are built to have as little of an environmental impact as possible while still giving visitors cozy and delightful lodgings.

Whatever your travel preferences or financial constraints, Portland offers a wide range of lodging options, each with its own special charm and character. Portland offers something for everyone, whether you're seeking for luxury, affordability, or sustainability.

Hotels

In recent years, the busy city of Portland, Oregon, has become a more popular travel destination. The city is renowned for its distinctive culture, delectable cuisine, and scenic surroundings. One of the most crucial factors to think about when making travel plans to Portland is where to stay. Fortunately, there are many different hotels in Portland to pick from, each with their own distinct charm and conveniences.

The downtown region of Portland is one of the most well-liked places to stay. Numerous of the city's top eateries, nightclubs, and retail establishments can be found here, along with well-liked destinations like Pioneer Courthouse Square and the Portland Art Museum. Portland's downtown is home to a wide variety of hotels, from high-end resorts to more affordable places to stay.

The Heathman Hotel is one of Portland's most recognizable lodgings. Since its establishment in the city in 1927, this historic inn has played host to a number of notable visitors, including President John F. Kennedy and the Dalai Lama. The Heathman Hotel is renowned for its opulent furnishings, first-rate amenities, and top-notch service. Food lovers frequently visit the hotel's Headwaters restaurant.

The Hi-Lo Hotel is a fantastic choice for anyone seeking a more contemporary hotel experience. With an emphasis on regional art and sustainability, this boutique hotel boasts a modern and elegant style. A few blocks from Pioneer Courthouse Square and the Portland Art Museum, the Hi-Lo Hotel is situated in the center of downtown Portland.

The Pearl District in Portland is another well-liked place for lodging. The chic eateries, boutique stores, and art galleries in this area are well-known. Many of Portland's top hotels, including the opulent Nines Hotel, are located in the Pearl District. The luxury hotel is housed in a former Meier & Frank department store, a landmark structure. The Nines Hotel offers some of the greatest dining in Portland, magnificent city views, a rooftop bar, and a restaurant.

There are numerous budget-friendly hotels in Portland as well for those on a tight budget. For those searching for a unique and entertaining hotel experience, the Jupiter Hotel is a fantastic choice. Unique, artistically built rooms, a courtyard with a fire pit, a well-liked bar, and a restaurant are all attractions of this hotel. The trendy East Burnside district, which is well-known for its nightlife and street art, is where you'll find the Jupiter Hotel.

When it comes to hotels, Portland has something to offer every kind of traveler. You're likely to discover something that suits your needs and interests, whether you're searching for an opulent escape, a chic boutique hotel, or a cost-effective choice. You can't go wrong when making travel plans to Portland as there are so many fantastic hotels to pick from.

Motels

Travelers have a wide variety of alternatives when it comes to lodging in Portland, Oregon. Motels are a popular option for tourists on a tight budget. For those wishing to tour the city on a budget, motels in Portland may be a more practical choice. It's crucial to keep in mind that not all hotels are made equal, so do your homework before reserving a space.

Along Interstate 5, one of Portland's most well-liked areas for lodging, are motels. Portland's downtown and other well-known tourist destinations are easily accessible from this neighborhood. Numerous motels along I-5 provide standard services like complimentary parking, Wi-Fi, and continental breakfast.

The Motel 6 Portland Central is a well-known motel in this region. This cost-effective choice provides straightforward, basic rooms at a reasonable price. The motel is a practical choice for people wishing to visit Portland on a budget because it is situated only a few miles from the city center.

The Palms Motel is another choice for guests on a tight budget. This motel is situated in the Montavilla district in Southeast Portland and provides tidy, cozy rooms at a reasonable cost. The Oregon Museum of Science and Industry and the Oregon Zoo are just a few miles from the Palms Motel, which is also close to many other well-known tourist destinations.

There are also some specialized motels in Portland for individuals seeking a more singular experience. The Jupiter NEXT, a popular lodging option, with rooms created by regional artists and a rooftop lounge with breathtaking city views. The trendy East Burnside district, which is well-known for its nightlife and street art, is where you'll find the Jupiter NEXT.

The Kennedy School is yet another themed hotel in Portland. This former school has been transformed into a distinctive hotel experience, and each of the rooms has a different theme. In addition, there are various pubs and restaurants, a movie theater, and a spa pool at The Kennedy School.

It's crucial to keep in mind that not all Portland motels are made equal, so do your research before making a reservation. Some motels might be known to draw particular kinds of tourists, have issues with cleanliness or safety, or all three. It's crucial to read reviews and make sure

Bed and breakfasts

Bed and breakfasts can be a great option for travelers searching for a more private and personalized lodging experience in Portland, Oregon. Compared to standard hotels, bed and breakfasts provide a more individualized experience, frequently with unique decor, home-cooked breakfasts, and hosts who are happy to provide recommendations for nearby restaurants and sights.

The Lion and the Rose Victorian Bed and Breakfast is a well-known bed and breakfast in Portland. The Irvington neighborhood is home to this ancient mansion, which offers magnificent, roomy accommodations with antique furniture and opulent extras. The Lion and the Rose is renowned for its friendly service and delectable breakfasts, which are served in the formal dining room on exquisite china.

The Bluebird Guesthouse in Portland is another well-liked bed and breakfast. This welcoming B&B offers comfortable rooms with eclectic design and friendly touches like baked cookies and fresh flowers. It is situated in the thriving Alberta Arts District. In addition, the Bluebird Guesthouse has a lovely garden and outdoor seating area that are ideal for unwinding with a book or a drink of wine.

The Portland International Guesthouse is a fantastic choice for anyone looking for a more contemporary bed and breakfast experience. This eco-friendly bed and breakfast is situated in the peaceful Beaumont-Wilshire neighborhood of Northeast Portland and offers modern furnishings, opulent amenities, and a sumptuous organic breakfast. Additionally, the Portland International Guesthouse provides a distinctive communal living area that is excellent for meeting other visitors and exchanging advice on the top Portland attractions.

Another well-liked alternative in Portland for those seeking a more individualized and private experience is The Fulton House Bed and Breakfast. This historic estate is situated in the peaceful Fulton district in Southwest Portland and offers opulent and roomy accommodations with contemporary conveniences like flat-screen TVs and whirlpool baths. The Fulton House is renowned for its friendly service and hearty cooked breakfasts created with seasonal, regional ingredients.

For travelers seeking a more secluded and comfortable lodging choice, bed & breakfasts in Portland can provide a distinctive and personalized experience. There are options to suit every traveler's preferences and budget, from cozy guesthouses to quaint estates. Make sure the bed and breakfast you choose satisfies your needs and preferences by reading reviews and looking at the property's website.

Hostels

Hostels in Portland can be a great option for those on a tight budget or those seeking a more communal and social lodging experience. Hostels provide individual rooms or shared dormitory-style accommodations at a lower cost than regular hotels, as well as chances to interact and meet other visitors.

The HI Portland Northwest Hostel is a well-liked hostel in Portland. The hostel, which is situated in the hip and storied Northwest neighborhood, provides inexpensive individual and dorm-style rooms. For travelers on a tight budget seeking a cozy and welcoming lodging alternative, the HI Portland Northwest Hostel is a perfect choice because it offers a shared kitchen, free Wi-Fi, and a large lounge space.

The Northwest Portland International Hostel is another well-liked hostel in Portland. The Pearl District, one of the city's liveliest and most pedestrian-friendly zones, is where you'll find this eco-friendly hostel. The Northwest Portland International Hostel has a range of lodging choices, including private rooms and shared dormitories, in addition to extras like a common kitchen, free Wi-Fi, and bike rental.

The Ace Hotel Portland can be a fantastic choice for individuals seeking a more distinctive and eccentric hostel experience. In the center of Portland, this boutique hotel and hostel offers warm, fashionable rooms with a vintage-inspired style. For those who enjoy music, the Ace Hotel Portland also has a community lounge room with a record player and a sizable vinyl collection.

The Mt. Hood International Hostel may be a fantastic choice for travelers seeking a more quiet and natural hostel experience. The hostel, which is situated near the picturesque Columbia River Gorge, provides both inexpensive shared dorm rooms and private rooms with breathtaking mountain views. Additionally, the Mt. Hood International Hostel offers access to hiking trails, a common kitchen, and a lounge area.

For budget-conscious tourists or those seeking a more private and communal experience, Portland's hostels can provide a cheap and sociable lodging alternative. There is something for every traveler's preferences and budget, from eco-friendly and boutique to quiet and nature-inspired. It's crucial to read reviews and look at the hostel's website before selecting one to make sure it suits your needs and interests.

Vacation Rentals

Vacation rentals can be a great option for travelers searching for a more flexible and at-home lodging option in Portland. With a vacation rental, you can have a more individualized and independent experience while staying in a private house or apartment, which frequently has a full kitchen and laundry facilities.

Airbnb is a well-known provider of holiday rentals in Portland. With thousands of listings around the city and its environs, Airbnb provides a wide range of accommodations, from little apartments to roomy houses. Airbnb is a terrific option for people seeking a more individualized and cozy experience because so many hosts provide personalized touches like local recommendations and welcome gifts.

Vacasa is yet another well-known vacation rental agency in Portland. Vacasa provides a wide range of possibilities for visitors of all budgets and interests with a vast selection of holiday homes and apartments in the city and nearby locations. Additionally, the business provides 24-hour customer service and a group of neighborhood property managers to make sure that visitors have a smooth and stress-free stay.

The River's Edge Retreat can be a fantastic choice for people seeking a more expensive and opulent vacation rental experience. This magnificent holiday property, which is situated on the Sandy River's banks, has four bedrooms, a gourmet kitchen, and a hot tub with breathtaking views of the river and surrounding mountains. The River's Edge getaway is a fantastic option for people wishing to combine a wilderness getaway with urban exploration because it is also only a short drive from downtown Portland.

The Caravan Tiny House Hotel can be a fantastic choice for vacationers seeking a more distinctive and eccentric holiday rental experience. Six tiny homes are included in this one-of-a-kind hotel, each having a distinctive interior decoration and design. The Caravan Tiny House Hotel is a fantastic option for tourists hoping to connect and socialize with other like-minded people because it also has a common lounge space and outdoor lounging area.

Portland vacation rentals can provide a more individualized and independent lodging alternative for travelers seeking a homelike setting. There is something to suit every traveler's preferences and budget, with choices ranging from modest apartments to opulent residences and distinctive little houses. To be sure that a vacation rental satisfies your needs and interests, it's crucial to read reviews and look at the property's website.

Boutique Inns

P ortland's boutique hotels are a great option for guests seeking a more distinctive and individualized lodging experience. Boutique hotels provide a more individualized and private experience, frequently with distinctive design and decor, custom facilities, and first-rate customer service.

The Jupiter NEXT, a well-known boutique hotel in Portland, is situated in the exciting and diverse East Burnside district and provides contemporary and elegant rooms with distinctive design components including neon artwork and bespoke murals. Along with a fitness center and free bike rentals, the hotel has a rooftop bar with breathtaking views of the city skyline.

The Ace Hotel is another well-liked boutique hotel in Portland. The Ace Hotel, which is in the center of

Portland's business district, offers comfortable, elegant rooms with a vintage-inspired design. Along with a coffee shop and bar serving regional craft beer and cocktails, the hotel also has a communal lounge area with a record player and a sizable vinyl collection.

The Kimpton RiverPlace Hotel can be a wonderful choice for individuals seeking a boutique hotel experience that is more environmentally friendly. The Kimpton RiverPlace Hotel, which is situated on the banks of the Willamette River, offers breathtaking views of the river and the mountains in the area in addition to a number of eco-friendly amenities like a complimentary hybrid car service and a program that encourages visitors to recycle and conserve water and energy.

The Sentinel Hotel can be a fantastic choice for guests seeking a more opulent and affluent boutique hotel experience. The Sentinel Hotel in downtown Portland is housed in a historic structure and offers opulent, spacious rooms with upscale features like marble bathrooms and fine linens. Along with a rooftop bar with expansive views of the city skyline, the hotel has a restaurant serving cuisine from the Pacific Northwest.

For visitors looking for a distinctive and fashionable experience, Portland's boutique hotels provide a more individualized and intimate lodging alternative. There are options to suit every traveler's preferences and budget, from eco-friendly and vintage-inspired to opulent and exquisite. It's crucial to read reviews and look at the hotel's website before selecting a boutique hotel to make sure it suits your needs and interests.

CHAPTER 4

Top Portland Attractions

The largest city in Oregon, Portland, is a bustling and eclectic destination that offers a distinctive fusion of scenic natural beauty, cultural landmarks, and contemporary conveniences. Portland is a city that has something to offer everyone, from its gorgeous parks and gardens to its renowned food and drink scene.

The International Rose Test Garden, which has over 7,000 rose plants and hundreds of species of roses, is one of the city's most well-known sights. The garden provides spectacular views of the city and the surrounding mountains and is the ideal place to stroll and take in the scented blooms.

The Portland Japanese Garden, which is regarded as one of the most authentic Japanese gardens outside of Japan, is another well-liked tourist attraction in Portland. Visitors can experience the peace and beauty of Japanese culture in this serene sanctuary of rich vegetation, water features, and traditional Japanese architecture.

Portland Museum of Art

One of the largest and oldest art museums in the Pacific Northwest is the Portland Art Museum. It was established in 1892 and has played a crucial role in shaping Portland's cultural scene for over a century. The museum is renowned for its magnificent collection of American, Asian, and European art as well as its dedication to promoting current and local artists.

It is situated in the center of downtown Portland, Oregon. We shall look into the collection, programs, and history of the Portland Art Museum in this essay.

When a group of regional artists and art aficionados founded the Portland Art Association in 1892, the Portland Art Museum's history began. The association wanted to introduce art to Portlanders and open a museum to display the city's expanding art collection. The Portland Art

Museum's first location was the Masonic Temple, which the association purchased in 1895. The museum has since relocated a number of times, growing its programming and collection with each relocation.

The historic Masonic Temple and the contemporary Mark Building, both of which opened in 2005, host the Portland Art Museum today. The Mark Building, created by the renowned firm Allied Works Architecture, is a spectacular example of modern architecture. The Masonic Temple's ancient beauty is well offset by the structure's modern contours and clean lines.

The museum's rich collection of American art is one of its main draws. The museum's collection of American art spans several centuries and contains pieces by some of the most well-known artists in the nation, including Georgia O'Keeffe, Winslow Homer, and John Singer Sargent. The collection also features a number of significant Northwest-produced works, such as creations by Mark Tobey, Morris Graves, and Sally Haley.

The Portland Art Museum has an amazing collection of Asian art in addition to its collection of American art. Asian artworks from China, Japan, Korea, and India that date back more than 5,000 years are included in the museum's collection. The collection's highlights include a large collection of Japanese woodblock prints and a sculpture of Vishnu made in Cambodia in the 12th century.

Additionally, the Portland Art Museum is dedicated to showcasing local and contemporary artists. Some of the most significant artists of the 20th and 21st centuries, such as Andy Warhol, Roy Lichtenstein, and Jasper Johns, have pieces in the museum's collection of contemporary art. The regional art collection of the museum emphasizes Northwest artists and features modern pieces by Marie Watt, Storm Tharp, and Brad Cloepfil, among others.

The Portland Art Museum is renowned for its comprehensive programming in addition to its excellent art collection. The museum hosts a variety of exhibitions, talks, and events all year long that are intended to appeal to visitors of all ages and interests. The education division of the museum provides classes, workshops, and summer camps for kids, youths, and adults.

The Northwest Film Center, which hosts numerous film screenings, festivals, and events all year long, is one of the museum's most well-liked activities. The film center has been a part of Portland's cultural scene for more than 40 years and boasts one of the biggest and most prestigious film programs in the nation.

Overall, the Portland Art Museum is a cultural treasure of the Pacific Northwest, boasting a rich and diversified collection of artwork, a dedication to promoting local and contemporary artists, and a wide range of programming created to pique the attention of visitors of all ages and interests. The Portland Art Museum is a must-see location with something to offer everyone, whether you're a local or a visitor to the area.

Pittock House

A historic home museum called Pittock Mansion may be found in Portland, Oregon, in the United States. The mansion is surrounded by 46 acres of forest and is set on a hilltop overlooking Portland. Henry Pittock, a well-known businessman and newspaper publisher, and his wife Georgiana commissioned the construction of the mansion in 1914. One of the best specimens of French Renaissance architecture in the country is thought to be the Pittock Mansion.

When Henry Pittock and his wife Georgiana first arrived in Portland in the late 19th century, the Pittock Mansion's history began. The Portland Daily Oregonian, the most significant newspaper in the state, was published by Henry Pittock. He had a big influence on Portland's growth and was essential to the city's development both economically and culturally.

Henry and Georgiana Pittock made the decision to erect a new house on a hilltop with a view of Portland in 1909.

The home was designed by Edward Foulkes, who was engaged by them, and work on it started in 1912. The neighborhood dubbed the 1914-built mansion "Pittock's Folly" because they felt it was too opulent and pricey for the couple's requirements.

The 46 acres of surrounding woodland area and 22 rooms make up the three-story Pittock Mansion. The palace was built in the early 20th century fashion known as French Renaissance. Sandstone makes up the mansion's facade, while Spanish tile covers the roof. Fine paintings, stylish furnishings, and other opulent elements fill the mansion's interior.

Up until 1958, when it was sold to the City of Portland, the Pittock family lived in the Pittock Mansion. The mansion was then turned into a museum and made one of Portland's most well-liked tourist destinations. Over 100,000 people visit the museum annually, and it is regarded as a significant piece of Portland's cultural heritage.

Over the years, the Pittock Mansion has undergone a number of renovations and restorations. The museum was enlarged in the 1960s to incorporate an orientation center, a gift shop, and more display space. The museum received a significant makeover in 2002 that brought the home back to its original state. The mansion's original wallpaper and carpeting were restored, and new heating, cooling, and electrical systems were installed as part of the refurbishment.

The Pittock Mansion is now a well-liked tourism attraction for both residents and visitors. Visitors can explore the mansion on their own and discover the Pitto family's history.

Portland Zoo

Animal lovers, environmentalists, and families seeking an engaging and instructive excursion frequently visit the Oregon Zoo. The 64-acre Portland Zoo in Oregon is home to more than 2,000 animals representing 260 different species. The zoo's goal is to motivate people to protect wildlife, and it accomplishes this through partnerships, initiatives, and exhibits.

One of the oldest zoos in the United States, the zoo was established in 1888. Richard Knight, a pharmacist who kept his animals in his backyard, first assembled it as a personal collection. After Knight's collection grew over time, the City of Portland accepted his donation and opened the zoo in its current location in 1959. The zoo has undergone numerous upgrades and additions throughout the years, including the refurbishment of current exhibits in addition to the creation of new ones.

The exhibits of the Oregon Zoo are divided up according to several continents, such as Africa, Asia, the Americas, and the Pacific Northwest. Each exhibit is made to mimic the creatures' native environments and instruct visitors about the species' habits, the necessity for conservation, and the dangers to which they are subject in the wild. The African Savanna, the Great Northwest, and the Polar Bears and

Penguins exhibit are among of the zoo's most well-liked exhibits.

Elephants, giraffes, lions, and zebras are just a few of the huge mammal species that may be found on the African Savanna. The display includes a miniature Kenyan village with a market, a school, and a house. The zoo's train, which rounds the African Savanna and provides a distinctive perspective on the animals, is also available for visitors to board.

The Pacific Northwest's flora and fauna, including grizzly bears, cougars, bald eagles, and river otters, are displayed in the Great Northwest exhibit. The display recreates the animals' native environment with a waterfall, pond, and forested area. Additionally, visitors can discover more about the native inhabitants of the area and how they interacted with the environment and animals.

One of the zoo's most well-liked attractions is the Polar Bears and Penguins exhibit, particularly in the sweltering summer months. The exhibit includes a pool where the polar bears can swim, a rocky beach where they can sunbathe, and an observation area where guests can watch the bears swim. The penguin exhibit has a pool, a beach, and a rocky environment. It is home to numerous species of penguins, including the well-known African penguin.

The Oregon Zoo provides a range of programs and activities for visitors of all ages in addition to its exhibits. The zoo's education division offers guided tours, animal interactions, and behind-the-scenes opportunities for kids and adults, as well as school programs, summer camps, and classes. The zoo also holds a number of events throughout the year, such as the beer tasting event BrewLights and the holiday light show ZooLights.

Additionally, the Oregon Zoo actively participates in regional and international conservation initiatives. The zoo takes involved in a number of breeding programs for endangered species, such as the Western pond turtle, Amur leopards, and California condors. The zoo also contributes to conservation and research initiatives in the Pacific Northwest, such as the Columbia Basin Pygmy Rabbit

Recovery Program and the Northern Spotted Owl Recovery Program. The zoo also collaborates with a number of conservation groups, such as the International Elephant Foundation, the Oregon Wild, and the Audubon Society of Portland.

A renowned institution in Portland, the Oregon Zoo is a prime example of a contemporary, educational, and conservation-oriented zoo. Its exhibitions, initiatives, and collaborations encourage the protection of wildlife, animal welfare, and the environment while giving visitors an enjoyable and interesting experience.

Japanese Garden in Portland

In the center of Portland, Oregon, there is a tranquil and lovely cultural destination called the Portland Japanese Garden. The 12-acre park, which was first established in 1963, has a variety of unique garden designs, including the Strolling Pond park, the Natural Garden, the Sand and Stone Garden, and the Flat Garden. The goal of the garden is to give a haven of beauty, peace, and harmony as well as to advance knowledge of and admiration for Japanese customs and culture.

Professor Takuma Tono, a Japanese landscape architect who was commissioned by the city of Portland to design a traditional Japanese garden, constructed the garden. A group of Japanese gardeners that Professor Tono brought with him toiled tirelessly for years to turn a hillside into a serene and lovely garden. Over 350,000 people visit the garden annually and it is now regarded as one of the most genuine Japanese gardens outside of Japan.

The Strolling Pond Garden, which may be seen from numerous vantage points along a winding route, is one of the most famous aspects of the Portland Japanese Garden. There is a waterfall, a tea house, and a sizable pond with numerous islands in the garden. In order to maintain appeal throughout the year, the plants in this garden were carefully chosen.

Flowering cherry trees, maples, and azaleas produce vibrant blossoms in the spring and summer, and evergreens and mosses foster a tranquil and meditative ambiance in the fall and winter.

Another highlight of the Portland Japanese Garden is the Natural Garden, which was created to look like the countryside of Japan. A network of streams and waterfalls, a pond, and a hillside covered in a mixture of evergreen, deciduous, and shrubbery are all characteristics of this landscape. The garden's paths wind through the vegetation, allowing guests to find unexpected vistas and tucked-away nooks.

The simple Sand and Stone Garden is a sizable area of raked sand and some strategically positioned rocks. Visitors are advised to concentrate on the patterns in the sand and the shapes of the rocks to discover a sense of quiet and stillness because this garden is intended to stimulate contemplation and meditation.

A variety of platforms and abstract sculptures make up The Flat Garden, a contemporary take on a traditional Japanese garden. A well-known Japanese landscape architect named

Hoichi Kurisu created this garden, fusing modern art and architecture with traditional Japanese design features.

The Portland Japanese Garden, in addition to its grounds, provides a number of cultural and educational activities all through the year, such as lessons in Japanese language, tea ceremony, calligraphy, and flower arranging. The garden also organizes a number of cultural celebrations, including the Tanabata Festival, the Cherry Blossom Festival, and the Japanese New Year's celebration.

The Portland Japanese Garden is dedicated to environmental care and sustainability. The infrastructure of the garden, including its structures and water elements, is created with sustainability and energy efficiency in mind. The garden also features a composting program to reduce waste and enhance soil health, and it uses a combination of organic and mechanical ways to handle pests and diseases.

A beautiful and serene haven in the middle of the city is the Portland Japanese Garden. For anybody interested in Japanese culture, landscape architecture, or just a moment of peace in a hectic world, this site is a must-see because of its thoughtfully planned gardens, cultural activities, and dedication to sustainability. A testament to the continuing allure of Japanese gardens and the ability of nature to uplift and comfort the human soul is the Portland Japanese Garden.

City of Books Powell

O ne of Portland, Oregon's most recognizable landmarks is Powell's City of Books. Tourists, book lovers, and voracious readers should all go there. The bookshop is renowned for its size, wide range of new and secondhand titles, and its distinctive environment that fosters an engaging reading experience.

The history of Powell's City of Books, its influence on the neighborhood of Portland, and the reasons it should be a must-see attraction for visitors to Portland will all be covered in this essay.

Walter Powell established Powell's City of Books in 1971. In a 1,000 square foot space in northwest Portland, it began as a modest bookstore. Used books were the focus of the establishment, Powell's Books. The bookshop grew over time to take up a full city block and more than 68,000 square feet, making it the largest independent bookstore in the entire world. In addition to an excellent selection of new and secondhand books, collectibles, and out-of-print books, the store contains over 3,500 categories.

The Portland neighborhood has been significantly impacted by Powell's City of Books. Visitors travel from all over the world to see this cultural landmark. It has also held several author events, book clubs, and literary festivals, making it a focus for literary and intellectual activity in Portland. The store has been mentioned in various articles, books, and movies, including the iconic TV series "Portlandia."

Additionally, Powell's City of Books has been essential in advancing literacy and helping regional communities. The bookshop is a helpful resource for students and teachers due to its wide collection of children's books, textbooks, and educational materials. To encourage reading and assist educational endeavors, the store also collaborates with nearby schools, libraries, and literacy initiatives.

Portland visitors should make time to explore Powell's City of Books. The bookstore provides a unique, immersive reading experience. The store's enormous selection of books offers hours of leisurely browsing for those looking for rare and obscure publications. With its quiet reading nooks, plush seats, and helpful staff, the bookstore has a distinctive ambience that makes book lovers feel at home.

In addition, Powell's City of Books provides tourists with guided tours that provide an inside look at the store's past, present, and collection. The bookstore also holds author gatherings and book signings, giving customers the chance to mingle with their favorite writers and discover fresh literary talent.

A Portland landmark, Powell's City of Books is now a must-see location for travelers, bookworms, and readers from all over the world. It is a cultural icon and an important source for literacy and education because to its huge book collection, distinctive ambience, and influence on the Portland neighborhood. Powell's City of Books is the ideal location for you whether you're a book aficionado seeking for your next great read or a tourist looking for a memorable experience.

Park Washington

Portland, Oregon's Washington Park is one of the most well-liked tourist attractions, and with good reason. It is a sizable urban park with more than 400 acres of land that is situated in Portland's West Hills. The park has a variety of activities, including museums and cultural organizations in addition to beautiful gardens and hiking trails.

We shall examine the various attributes and attractions that make Washington Park a must-visit location for tourists in Portland in this essay.

The wealth of natural beauty in Washington Park is one of its most outstanding characteristics. Several gardens, each with a special charm of their own, can be found in the park. With over 10,000 rose bushes in over 650 different kinds, the International Rose Test Garden is a particularly well-liked tourist destination.

The garden is a must-see for anybody traveling to Portland from May to September when it is in bloom. Another highlight of the park is the Japanese Garden, which has elegant ponds, beautifully tended plants that depict the four seasons, and traditional Japanese architecture. A well-liked attraction for both families and animal enthusiasts is the Oregon Zoo, which is housed within the park and has a variety of species from throughout the world.

There are many hiking routes in Washington Park that provide breathtaking views of the city and the surrounding countryside for individuals who appreciate the outdoors and trekking. Visitors can enjoy the natural beauty of the Pacific Northwest on the 30-mile Wildwood Trail, which passes through the park and links to Forest Park. Another well-liked destination for hiking is the Hoyt Arboretum, which is a part of the park and has more than 2,000 different kinds of trees and plants.

Washington Park includes a number of cultural institutions that provide tourists an insight into the history and culture of the area in addition to its natural attractions. Families like visiting the Portland Children's Museum, which features engaging exhibits that promote both learning and play.

Another well-liked destination is the World Forestry Center, which has displays exploring the background and significance of forestry in the Pacific Northwest. The park's Oregon Holocaust Memorial serves as a solemn reminder of the Holocaust's atrocities and a memorial to those who perished during them.

The Oregon Zoo Summer Concert Series and the Portland Japanese Garden's Autumn Moon Festival are two other annual events that take place in Washington Park. These activities offer a fun and exciting way to see the park's cultural institutions and natural splendor.

For anyone traveling to Portland, Washington Park is a must-see location. It is a must-visit location for travelers of all ages because of its natural beauty, cultural institutions, and variety of attractions. Washington Park includes activities for all interests, including hiking, gardens, museums, and cultural events. In order to appreciate the beauty and diversity of this excellent urban park, be sure to include Washington Park on your schedule the next time you're in Portland.

Lan Su Chinese Garden

The Lan Su Chinese Garden, one of the most beautiful Chinese gardens in the nation, is located in Portland, Oregon. This lovely garden, also known as the Garden of the Awakening Orchids, is an oasis in the middle of the city, providing guests with a tranquil respite and a window into Chinese culture and history. We'll go through the various qualities and highlights that make Portland's Lan Su Chinese Garden a must-visit location in this post.

In Portland's Old Town Chinatown district, there is a walled garden called the Lan Su Chinese Garden that takes almost a full city block. The garden has an unmistakable impression of elegance and beauty because it was made using materials that were imported directly from China and was designed by Chinese artists. Since its public opening in 2000, the garden has grown to become one of the most well-liked tourist destinations in the city.

The garden's architectural layout is one of its most stunning aspects. The garden is split up into a number of distinct sections, each with its own special attributes and attractions. The central lake, which is the garden's focal point and is encircled by lush flora, winding pathways, and an exquisite teahouse, is its focal point. The intricately crafted pavilions, bridges, and rock formations that make up the garden's scenery can be seen as visitors meander along the paths.

The variety of plants and trees at the Lan Su Chinese Garden is another highlight. Bamboo, lotus, magnolia, and many other Chinese trees and plants may be seen in the garden. These plants are set out in the manner of a traditional Chinese garden, with special consideration paid to their positioning and the relationships they form with one another.

These plants and trees are beautiful all throughout the year since they change with the seasons and give a variety of hues and textures. The Lan Su Chinese Garden offers a range of educational programs and events for anyone who want to learn more about Chinese culture and tradition.

These activities are intended to provide visitors a richer experience and a better knowledge of the significance and history of the garden. A traditional tea ceremony, a course on Chinese calligraphy, or a tour of the garden are all available to guests.

The garden also holds a number of occasions throughout the year, such as the Moon Festival and the Chinese New

Year celebration. Visitors have the opportunity to explore Chinese culture and heritage at these events in a fun-loving setting. The garden is covered with lanterns, vibrant banners, and other traditional decorations during these occasions, and guests can take part in live performances, food, and other activities.

Anyone traveling to Portland must see the Lan Su Chinese Garden. Visitors of all ages will have an amazing experience because to its spectacular architecture, gorgeous plants, and informative programs. The Lan Su Chinese Garden is certain to make an impression on anyone with an interest in Chinese culture, gardens, or just looking for a quiet hideaway in the middle of the city.

Therefore, be sure to include the Lan Su Chinese Garden in your itinerary the next time you're in Portland so that you can enjoy its beauty and serenity.

Garden of International Rose Tests

T here are several parks and gardens in Portland, Oregon, but maybe none are as well-known as the International Rose Test Garden. The Rose landscape in Portland's West Hills is a breathtaking 4.5-acre landscape where more than 7,000 rose plants representing more than 550 different rose kinds can be found

. The International Rose Test Garden is one of Portland's top tourist attractions, and we'll look at all of its varied characteristics and attractions in this essay.

One of the nation's oldest rose gardens, the International Rose Test Garden was founded in 1917. Today, the garden is a popular destination for tourists from all over the world, who come to admire the stunning beauty of the rose plants and to learn about their history and significance. It was established as a means of preserving European rose varieties that were threatened during World War I.

The International Rose Test Garden's vastness is one of its most outstanding characteristics. Each of the several portions of the garden has its own special characteristics and attractions. Visitors can meander through the various parts and take in the various rose kinds that are displayed in vibrant beds and surrounded by luxuriant vegetation. A number of fountains, sculptures, and other decorative elements are also present in the garden, which further enhances its beauty and elegance.

The variety of roses in the International Rose Test Garden is another highlight. Over 550 different rose varieties can be found in the garden, which is divided into groups based on the traits and qualities of each variety. Grandifloras, floribundas, hybrid tea roses, and other types, each with its own distinctive colors and shapes, are available for visitors to enjoy their beauty and smell.

The garden also has a separate area just for miniature roses, which are ideal for people who want to appreciate rose beauty in a more constrained setting.

The International Rose Test Garden offers a range of educational programs and events for anyone who want to learn more about roses. With the help of these programs, guests will gain a deeper appreciation of the rose's significance in history as well as useful advice for growing and caring for roses at home. Visitors can take a tour with a guide, attend a lesson on pruning or propagating roses, or participate in a celebration with a rose theme, such the Rose Festival or the Rose City Classic Dog Show.

The International Rose Test Garden is also a well-liked venue for weddings and other special occasions. It is the perfect setting for outdoor weddings, picture sessions, and other special occasions due to its breathtaking beauty and opulent surrounds. The garden's employees can offer suggestions for regional suppliers and services as well as assistance with planning and logistics.

Anyone visiting Portland should make sure to visit the International Rose Test Garden. Visitors of all ages will have an unforgettable experience thanks to its spectacular beauty, extensive history, and educational offerings. The

International Rose Test Garden is certain to make an impact, whether you're a fan of roses, gardens, or simply seeking a quiet hideaway in the middle of the city. In order to appreciate the beauty and serenity of this exceptional destination, make sure to include a visit to the International Rose Test Garden on your agenda the next time you're in Portland.

CHAPTER 5

Portland Outdoor Activities

T he city of Portland, Oregon, is well-known for its stunning natural surroundings, which include imposing mountains, meandering rivers, and lush forests. Portland is a great place for outdoor activities of many types, from hiking and bicycling to kayaking and fishing, thanks to its temperate climate and abundance of green spaces.

There are many parks in the city itself, including the well-known Forest Park, which spans more than 5,000 acres and has miles of hiking and bike routes. Another well-liked vacation spot is Washington Park, which has places to go including the Oregon Zoo, Hoyt Arboretum, and the Portland Japanese Garden.

Outside the city limits, the surrounding area offers a plethora of chances for outdoor adventure. While Mount Hood, just an hour's drive away, offers some of the best skiing and snowboarding in the Pacific Northwest, the Columbia River Gorge, east of Portland, offers world-class hiking, windsurfing, and kiteboarding opportunities.

With its large network of bike-friendly streets and bike lanes across the city, Portland is also a mecca for cyclists. Bicyclists, joggers, and walkers all love the Springwater Corridor, a 40-mile paved trail that connects Portland to the suburbs of Gresham and Boring.

With options for kayaking, paddleboarding, and fishing along the Willamette and Columbia Rivers, water enthusiasts will never run out of things to do in and near Portland. The Oregon Coast, with its picturesque beaches and rugged shoreline ideal for hiking, surfing, and whale watching, is only a couple of hours' drive away for those seeking to escape the city.

Portland provides a multitude of possibilities to discover the natural beauty of the Pacific Northwest, regardless of whether you're an experienced outdoor enthusiast or simply looking to enjoy some fresh air and exercise. There is something for everyone in this busy and scenic city, from tranquil hikes through old-growth forests to heart-pounding activities on the sea.

Trails for biking and hiking

The tremendous natural beauty of Portland, Oregon is well recognized, and hiking and bicycling are two of the best ways to take it all in. Portland has developed into a popular destination for outdoor enthusiasts of all ability levels because to its wide network of parks and trails around the city and its surroundings. We'll look at why Portland's hiking and bike trails are such a draw for visitors in this essay.

The abundance of open spaces in Portland is one of the key factors contributing to the city's popularity of hiking and bike paths. Portland features parks for everyone, from the larger Forest Park, which has over 5,000 acres and miles of hiking and bike trails, to the more compact but no less stunning Laurelhurst Park. Whether they want to go on a strenuous walk or a leisurely bike ride, these parks give visitors an opportunity to get away from the bustle of the city and experience nature.

Portland is bordered by some of the most breathtaking natural settings in the Pacific Northwest in addition to the parks inside the city limits. A short drive from the city center, the Columbia River Gorge has some of the best hiking and biking trails in the area, with breathtaking vistas of waterfalls, cliffs, and forests.

One hour's drive from Portland is Mount Hood, the highest point in Oregon, which offers some of the best skiing and snowboarding in the Pacific Northwest in the winter.

The fact that Portland has made significant investments in building an infrastructure that supports outdoor recreation is another factor contributing to the popularity of the city's hiking and bike trails. The Springwater Corridor, a 40-mile paved track that connects Portland to the suburbs of Gresham and Boring, is a favorite with bikers, joggers, and walkers alike. The Springwater Corridor's wide network of bike lanes and bike-friendly streets make it simple for tourists to explore the city by bike.

For visitors' convenience and enjoyment, the city has also invested in creating new trails and enhancing old ones. For instance, the Banks-Vernonia State route, a 21-mile paved route that goes through some of Oregon's most stunning natural settings, including forests, farmland, and wetlands, is situated just west of Portland. The city has also attempted to make more parks and trails wheelchair accessible for those with impairments.

Last but not least, Portland's hiking and bike trails are well-liked because they provide tourists an opportunity to interact with nature and experience the natural splendor of the Pacific Northwest firsthand. Visitors visiting Portland can immerse themselves in the area's natural beauty and experience a sense of amazement and wonder that can be challenging to find in other parts of the country whether trekking through old-growth forests or biking along the banks of the Columbia River.

Due to the city's extensive network of green spaces, its proximity to beautiful natural landscapes, its investment in outdoor recreation infrastructure, and the opportunity they provide visitors to connect with nature, hiking and biking trails are a major draw for tourists in Portland. Portland's hiking and biking trails are sure to deliver an unforgettable experience, whether you're an experienced outdoor lover or just seeking to get some fresh air and exercise.

Forest Park

With a total area of more than 5,000 acres, Portland, Oregon's Forest Park is one of the country's biggest urban parks. The park is a well-liked destination for both residents and visitors, providing a tranquil escape from the busy metropolis with miles of hiking and bike paths, animals, and stunning landscape. This essay will examine the origins and relevance of Portland's Forest Park as a tourist destination.

Following years of efforts by locals to preserve the area's natural beauty, Forest Park was created in 1948. The park was built using a mix of public and private funds, with the city of Portland buying land and private donors donating plots of land to the park. The Portland Parks & Recreation Department currently owns and operates Forest Park, working to preserve the park's natural beauty and safeguard its flora and fauna.

The wide path network in Forest Park is one of its most noteworthy features. Over 80 miles of trails in the park offer everything from leisurely strolls to strenuous hikes.

These routes give visitors the opportunity to discover the park's natural splendor while also getting some exercise as they wind through dense forests, along bubbling streams, and up steep hillsides. Popular paths include the Wildwood Trail, which winds through the center of the city for more than 30 miles.

Park at Tom McCall Waterfront

Portland, Oregon's Tom McCall Waterfront Park is a well-known destination that welcomes tourists from all over the world. This 36-acre park, which bears the name of the previous governor of the state, is situated on the Willamette River's west bank. It is a lovely location with a wide range of attractions, events, and recreational opportunities. We shall examine the many advantages and attractions of Tom McCall Waterfront Park in this essay.

The magnificent views of the city skyline and the Willamette River are one of this park's standout qualities. Visitors can unwind in the park's lush green areas or wander along the riverbank paths and take in the breathtaking landscape. The park is kept up well and has a variety of trees, flowers, and other greenery, giving visitors a peaceful environment to enjoy.

There are numerous outdoor pursuits in Tom McCall Waterfront Park that draw visitors of all ages. There are numerous playgrounds and open fields in the park where people can picnic, fly kites, and play sports. Fitness buffs enjoy using the park's bike routes and running trails, and the riverfront promenade is a fantastic area for leisurely strolls. The park also contains a number of boat docks that give visitors access to the Willamette River for boating and fishing.

In addition to offering recreational opportunities, Tom McCall Waterfront Park serves as the venue for several events all year long. Numerous festivals, concerts, and other events are held in the park that are well-attended. For instance, the park hosts the well-known Waterfront Blues Festival each year, which includes live music, food vendors, and other attractions. The Portland Saturday Market, a venerable institution that draws artisans and sellers from all over the Pacific Northwest, is also held in the park.

Tom McCall Waterfront Park's proximity to other points of interest in Portland, Oregon, is a significant draw as well. The Portland Art Museum, the Oregon Historical Society

Museum, and the Portland Japanese Garden are just a short stroll away for visitors. The park is a handy location for those who want to explore the city because so many eateries, cafes, and stores are close by.

In addition to its many attractions, Tom McCall Waterfront Park offers the city of Portland a number of useful advantages. The park offers a lovely green space in the middle of the city, which enhances the quality of life for locals. Additionally, it helps the local economy by luring visitors and hosting events that generate income for nearby companies.

Tom McCall Waterfront Park is an important component of Portland's downtown, providing both tourists and locals with a variety of attractions and advantages. The park offers something for everyone, from its breathtaking views of the city skyline and riverfront to its many recreational opportunities and events. As a result, it should come as no surprise that it is one of Portland's most cherished and well-liked attractions and a must-see location for visitors.

Portland Saturday market

One of the city's most well-liked attractions, Portland Saturday Market attracts tourists from all over the world. The market, which is housed in the city's Old Town district, has approximately 250 regional food, craft, and art sellers. The many factors that make the Portland Saturday Market such a popular tourist destination will be discussed in this essay.

The large selection of goods available at the Portland Saturday Market is one of its most distinctive qualities. Visitors can browse through a staggering selection of handmade goods, including ceramics, woodwork, clothes, jewelry, and other articles of clothing.

The market is also home to a large number of food vendors serving a wide range of cuisine, including Thai, Mexican, and Middle Eastern dishes. There is something for everyone to enjoy at the Saturday market in Portland because to the range of offers.

The merry and boisterous ambiance at Portland Saturday Market is another key draw. The market is renowned for its upbeat and friendly atmosphere, which is enhanced by live music and street performers. While they shop and eat, visitors can take in the sounds of regional musicians, creating a distinctive and memorable experience. The market has a diverse mixture of locals and visitors mixing together, making it a terrific area to people-watch.

Supporting regional companies and artists can also be done at the Portland Saturday Market. The market is a fantastic way to find new and up-and-coming artists and support the neighborhood economy because all of the sellers are local to the Portland area. Visitors can interact with the artists and craftspeople, learn about their processes, and buy unique goods that aren't available anyplace else.

Tourists are drawn to Portland Saturday Market because of its location. The market's location on the Willamette River's banks offers stunning views of the river and its surroundings. Many other well-known Portland attractions, including the Portland Art Museum, the Oregon Historical

Society Museum, and the Portland Japanese Garden, are also accessible by foot from the market. Portland Saturday Market is a great starting point for a day-long exploration of the city's downtown by tourists.

The chance to explore Portland's distinctive culture and community is another key draw of the Saturday Market there. The market's concentration on handcrafted and locally sourced goods perfectly captures the quirky and inventive spirit of the city. By interacting with the vendors and taking in the market's vibrant and diverse culture, visitors can get a sense of the city's values and attitudes.

The Portland Saturday Market is a must-see destination for visitors to the area. It provides a wholly distinctive and genuine Portland experience with its broad selection of goods, jovial environment, and emphasis on local companies and culture. Portland Saturday Market is the ideal place to go if people are searching for a one-of-a-kind souvenir, a tasty lunch, or just a fun and memorable day out.

Wine Tasting

Many cities, including Portland, Oregon, offer wine tasting as a popular attraction. Portland has a range of options for visitors to try some of the best wines in the Pacific Northwest due to its closeness to the Willamette Valley, one of the top wine areas in the world. We will examine the many factors that make wine tasting such a popular activity in Portland in this essay.

The range of wineries and vineyards that can be visited is one of Portland's wine tasting's standout characteristics. Over 500 wineries can be found in the Willamette Valley, many of which are close to Portland.

Visitors have a variety of options, including smaller family-run wineries, boutique vineyards, and bigger commercial enterprises, each of which offers a distinctive experience and the possibility to sample various wines. Numerous of these wineries also provide tours where guests can learn about the history of the area and the winemaking process.

The chance to sample some of the best wines in the world is a significant draw of wine tasting in Portland. The Pinot Noir wines produced in the Willamette Valley are acknowledged as some of the best in the world. Chardonnay, Riesling, and Syrah are among additional well-liked grape varieties in the area. Wine enthusiasts can try a variety of these wines, some of which are only offered in very small numbers or only at the winery.

Portland's natural beauty and surroundings can be enjoyed while wine tasting as well. The surrounding hills and valleys may be seen beautifully from many of the wineries and vineyards, which are situated in scenic areas. A genuinely unique and tranquil experience can be had by visitors while sipping wine and admiring the scenery.

Additionally, Portland wine tasting provides an opportunity to discover the history and culture of the area. Since many of the wineries and vineyards are family-run and have been in business for generations, they can shed light on the Willamette Valley's winemaking traditions and history. Visitors can learn about the region's unusual terroir and climate, as well as how these elements affect the specific flavors and qualities of the wines made there.

Meeting and interacting with other wine enthusiasts is yet another great benefit of wine tasting in Portland. Wineries and tasting rooms offer a laid-back atmosphere where guests can mingle with like-minded individuals, exchange knowledge, and share their experiences. For many guests, this sense of belonging and camaraderie is a big lure, and it also increases how much fun they have while there.

Last but not least, going wine tasting in Portland is a fantastic way to boost the local economy and companies. Since many of the wineries and vineyards are modest, family-run businesses, visiting them benefits the neighborhood. Additionally, wine tourism is a sizable source of income for the area and supports the expansion and advancement of the regional economy.

Portland's well-liked wine tasting destination provides guests with a distinctive and enjoyable experience. It is no surprise that wine tasting has grown to be such a popular pastime in the city given its diversity of wineries and vineyards, stunning scenery, rich history and culture, and sense of community. Wine tasting in Portland is a memorable event that should not be missed, regardless of whether visitors are wine experts or just seeking for a leisurely and interesting day out.

CHAPTER 6

Neighborhoods in Portland

Portland, Oregon is renowned for its distinctive and varied neighborhoods, each of which has its own special charm and personality. Portland's neighborhoods offer a wide range of experiences for locals and visitors alike, from historic districts to hip urban enclaves.

The Pearl District, a popular area of Portland, is situated in the center of the city. The Pearl District, which was formerly an industrial region, has been turned into a vibrant residential and business district with chic eateries, shops, and art galleries. The region is a well-liked location for outdoor leisure as a result of the presence of several well-known parks, including Tanner Springs Park and Jamison Square.

Hawthorne, which can be found in the southeast of the city, is yet another well-liked area in Portland. Hawthorne, which is well-known for its unique mix of stores, eateries, and bars, is a haven for foodies and vintage shoppers. A strong sense of community can also be found in the area, which hosts a lot of annual festivals and local events.

Another well-liked Portland neighborhood is the Alberta Arts District, which is renowned for its colorful street art and regional art galleries. The district, which is in the northeastern portion of the city, is home to a number of well-known eateries and nightclubs as well as a thriving farmers market on weekends.

Laurelhurst is a popular option for people looking for a more tranquil neighborhood with less noise. Laurelhurst, a neighborhood in the east of the city, is renowned for its tree-lined avenues, old homes, and welcoming atmosphere for families. Laurelhurst Park, a well-liked location for picnics, playgrounds, and outdoor performances, is also located in the neighborhood.

The Alphabet District, which is found in the northwest of the city, is one of Portland's oldest neighborhoods. Along with its hip restaurants and shops, the neighborhood is renowned for its historic residences and architectural style. A number of well-liked parks, including one of the biggest urban woods in the nation, Forest Park, are also located in the Alphabet District.

Portland's communities are different in terms of affordability in addition to culture and atmosphere. There are numerous districts in Portland that provide more inexpensive living alternatives and a more laid-back attitude, despite the fact that other neighborhoods, including the Pearl District and the Alphabet District, are well known for their high-end mansions and costly restaurants.

St. Johns, which lies in the city's north, is one such neighborhood. St. Johns, which is well known for having working-class beginnings, has a vibrant local arts scene and a strong feeling of community. The St. Johns Farmers Market and a number of well-known food carts make the area a favorite among foodies.

Montavilla, which is a reasonably priced neighborhood in Portland, is situated in the southeast of the city. Montavilla is renowned for its eclectic mix of old and new buildings, as well as for its exciting street fairs and festivals. Along with several well-known eateries and bars, the area is also home to a vintage movie theater.

Portland's downtown

In the center of Portland, Oregon, is the thriving and busy neighborhood known as Downtown Portland. Some of the city's most recognizable landmarks and attractions are located there, making it a center for commerce, culture, and entertainment. We will examine the history, culture, and personality of Downtown Portland in this essay and talk about why it is such a cherished area for both residents and tourists.

The Background of Portland's Downtown

Francis Pettygrove, the city's first mayor, named Portland after Portland, Maine, when it was established in 1851.

Many of the oldest buildings in downtown Portland, which was one of the first areas to be developed, were constructed in the late 1800s and early 1900s. These structures, which were mostly composed of brick and stone, reflect the Beaux-Arts, Art Deco, and Gothic Revival architectural movements of the time with their elaborate façade and minute details.

Early in the 20th century, banks, department shops, and other enterprises established themselves in Downtown Portland, making it a hub for trade and industry. The 15-story Elks Building, the city's first skyscraper, was constructed in 1912, and numerous others followed. However, by the middle of the 20th century, a lot of businesses had relocated to the suburbs, and Downtown Portland was in disrepair.

The local government started making significant investments in Downtown Portland in the 1970s and 1980s,

District of Pearl

In the center of Portland, Oregon, there is a thriving and affluent district called The Pearl District. Over the past few decades, the area has undergone significant redevelopment and revitalization, evolving from a grimy industrial district to one of Portland's most coveted neighborhoods. The Pearl District, which is renowned for its chic boutiques, posh restaurants, and exciting nightlife, has emerged as a center for art, culture, cuisine, and entertainment.

History of Pearl District

A number of companies, warehouses, and railroad yards originally occupied the Pearl District, which was a busy industrial neighborhood. After being originally populated in the 1860s, the region developed into a significant manufacturing base for the city by the early 20th century. The Pearl Brewery, which opened in the early 1900s and made beer until the 1970s, gave the area its name. The region was completely abandoned and in decay in the 1970s and 1980s.

The city of Portland started making investments in the Pearl District's redevelopment in the 1990s. Many of the old warehouses and factories were transformed by the city into chic loft apartments, art galleries, and high-end shopping areas. Young professionals and artists were attracted to the region by its industrial appeal and proximity to downtown Portland, and it quickly gained popularity among them.

The Pearl District, one of Portland's most coveted areas today, is renowned for its upscale retail, cutting-edge dining, and vibrant nightlife.

Living in the Pearl District

The Pearl District is renowned for its upmarket loft condominiums and flats, which provide inhabitants with a distinctive fusion of modern conveniences and industrial charm. Many of the area's historic structures have been transformed into roomy loft apartments, which feature exposed brick walls, high ceilings, and sizable windows with breathtaking city views.

A number of upscale condominium buildings can be found in the Pearl District, many of which provide opulent amenities including rooftop pools, exercise centers, and round-the-clock concierge services. The Pearl District is well-liked by young professionals and families who value the neighborhood's urban ambiance and near proximity to downtown Portland, despite the high expense of living there.

Dining and shopping in the Pearl District

The Pearl District is renowned for its upscale stores and fashionable boutiques. Many regional and national retailers can be found in the area, selling everything from designer clothing and accessories to home furnishings and specialty foods. The neighborhood's beauty and character are enhanced by the fact that many of the local businesses are housed in old structures.

With so many restaurants, cafes, and pubs to select from, the Pearl District is certainly a foodie's dream. The neighborhood is well-known for its upmarket eating scene, and many of the greatest restaurants in the city are found there. The Pearl District has plenty to offer every pallet, from hip sushi bars and French bistros to quaint cafés and artisanal bakeries.

Cultural Activities in the Pearl District

There are many galleries and museums in the Pearl District, which has a thriving arts and cultural scene. The Portland Art Museum, which has over 42,000 works of art in its collection, including works by current artists and antiquity from all over the world, is located in the neighborhood.

A number of sculptures and murals can be found all across the Pearl District, which is well-known for its public art displays. A number of galleries and studios that display the work of regional and international artists are located in the area.

The Pearl District in Portland has grown to be one of the most sought-after areas to live, work, and play. It is a distinctive and energetic neighborhood. Young professionals, families, and tourists all enjoy visiting this region because of its long history, charming industrial aesthetic, and close access to downtown Portland. With its upscale stores, cutting-edge eateries, and growing

Alberta Arts District

In Portland, Oregon, there is a vibrant and diversified area known as the Alberta Arts District that is well-known for its vibrant arts scene. Martin Luther King Jr. Boulevard borders the Alberta Arts District, which is situated in northeast Portland. Boulevard, Northeast 33rd Avenue, Northeast Ainsworth Street, and Northeast Killingsworth Street are to the west, east, north, and south, respectively.

There are numerous eateries, cafes, bars, and businesses in the Alberta Arts District that provide a distinctive fusion of regional and global flavors. The region is particularly well-known for its food carts, which provide anything from Ethiopian injera to Vietnamese banh mi. A number of craft breweries, including Great Notion Brewing and StormBreaker Brewing, are also located in the area and provide a variety of regional beers and seasonal specialties.

The Alberta Arts District's thriving arts sector is one of its key draws. There are various galleries and studios in the area, as well as a number of yearly art events including the Last Thursday street festival.

This festival of regional artists, musicians, and performers happens on the last Thursday of every month from May through September. During Last Thursday, pedestrians are free to explore the many vendors and performers who line the sidewalks while the streets are closed to cars.

The Alberta cultural District is renowned for its community action and engagement in addition to its cultural sector. The area has a long history of encouraging sustainable development and patronizing community businesses. A community-based organization called Alberta Main Street, which was established in 2009, strives to support neighborhood redevelopment and economic growth in the Alberta Arts District.

The group provides a variety of services, such as business development and marketing aid, to support neighborhood companies and highlight their distinctive qualities.

The rich history and cultural diversity of the Alberta Arts District are crucial additional features. African American families first moved to the area in the early 20th century, and throughout its existence it has served as a hub for African American culture and community. The area continues to be a centre of cultural interchange and understanding even though it is now home to a varied variety of inhabitants from various socioeconomic and racial origins.

Despite its many advantages, gentrification and rising housing costs have recently presented problems for the Alberta Arts District. Many long-time residents have been forced to move out as the area has grown more popular and desirable as a result of rising rents and property values. This has raised worries about the neighborhood's cultural character being lost and the most vulnerable inhabitants being evicted.

Despite these difficulties, the Alberta Arts District is still a thriving and distinctive community that both locals and tourists adore. It serves as an example of sustainable and inclusive development in Portland and beyond thanks to its unique blend of art, culture, and community involvement.

The Alberta Arts District is undoubtedly worthwhile a visit if you're searching for a delicious meal, an original work of art, or a lively cultural experience.

Mississippi Avenue

Portland, Oregon's Mississippi Avenue neighborhood is a thriving and colorful area renowned for its distinctive personality and multicultural population. Mississippi Avenue, which is part of the North Portland neighborhood, runs from North Fremont Street to North Skidmore Street and is dotted with a number of stores, eateries, pubs, and community centers.

Beginning in the early 20th century, Mississippi Avenue has a long and illustrious history. The area, which was initially populated by Irish and German immigrants, previously served as a center for business and industry, with a number of factories and warehouses lining the streets. However, the area deteriorated over time, and by the 1970s it was a dilapidated and abandoned area.

Mississippi Avenue, however, started to undergo a renaissance in the 1990s as a result of the influx of young professionals, musicians, and artists. The area is now renowned for its active street life, strong arts sector, and community involvement.

The wide variety of stores, eateries, and bars on Mississippi Avenue is one of its key draws. Numerous independent boutiques and vintage stores, as well as a number of regional breweries and cider houses, can be found in the neighborhood. Miss Delta serves barbecue in the South, whereas Homegrown Smoker serves vegan Mexican food. A number of bakeries and coffee businesses, including the well-known Blue Star Donuts, are also located in the neighborhood.

Mississippi Avenue is renowned for its arts and culture scene in addition to its selection of food and beverages. Numerous music venues, such as Mississippi Studios and the Alberta Rose Theatre, as well as several art galleries, such as Land Gallery and Guardino Gallery, are located in the neighborhood.

The area also organizes a number of yearly events that highlight the neighborhood's various artistic abilities, including the Mississippi Street Fair and the PorchFest music festival.

Mississippi Avenue's involvement in and action for the neighborhood is another significant feature. The area has a long history of encouraging sustainable development and patronizing community businesses. The Mississippi Avenue Business Association, for instance, promotes neighborhood economic growth and civic involvement through programs like the Mississippi Marketplace, a weekly farmers market with regional producers and food carts.

Mississippi Avenue is also home to a multicultural neighborhood that captures the distinctive spirit of the area. Along with many other ethnic and socioeconomic groups, there are many African Americans living in the area. The neighborhood's many community places, including the Mississippi Street Fair, which showcases a broad selection of cuisine, music, and art from all over the world, celebrate this diversity.

Mississippi Avenue has numerous advantages, but it also has some drawbacks. Concerns concerning the eviction of longtime inhabitants and the destruction of the neighborhood's cultural character have arisen as a result of rising housing costs and gentrification.

Through programs like the Mississippi Avenue Housing Coalition, which promotes affordable housing and equitable development in the neighborhood, the community is attempting to address these problems.

The best of Portland's arts, culture, and community involvement are on display in the distinctive and energetic neighborhood of Mississippi Avenue. It serves as a role model for inclusive and equitable urban development due to its wide variety of stores, eateries, and community spaces, as well as its long history and dedication to sustainable development.

Mississippi Avenue offers something for everyone, whether you're looking for a delicious lunch, a one-of-a-kind shopping experience, or an exciting cultural event.

Hawthorne neighborhood

Portland, Oregon's popular Hawthorne District is renowned for its varied mix of local shops, distinctive architecture, and lively neighborhood. Southeast Portland's Hawthorne Avenue, which runs from SE 12th to SE 60th, is home to a variety of stores, eateries, pubs, and public gathering places.

When it was a thriving commercial hub in the early 20th century, Hawthorne Avenue has a long and illustrious history. The avenue, which was formerly known as Asylum Avenue, connected to the Oregon State Hospital. The route was renamed Nathaniel Hawthorne route in the 1920s, and as time went on, it flourished as a residential and commercial district.

The Hawthorne District is currently renowned for its mixed community and active street life. Its distinctive personality is established by the assortment of historic residences and structures that line the street as well as the numerous locally owned businesses that call the area home.

The broad selection of stores, eateries, and bars in the Hawthorne District is one of its main draws. Numerous independent boutiques and vintage stores, as well as a number of regional breweries and cider houses, can be found in the neighborhood. Aviv serves vegan comfort food, whereas Bread and Ink Café serves traditional American cuisine.

A number of bakeries and coffee businesses, including the well-known Blue Star Donuts, are also located in the neighborhood. The Hawthorne District is renowned for its arts and culture scene in addition to its selection of food and beverages.

Numerous music venues, such as the Hawthorne Theatre and the Clinton Street Theater, as well as several art galleries, such as the Pushdot Studio and the Mark Woolley Gallery, are located in the neighborhood. The area also hosts a number of yearly events that highlight the neighborhood's various artistic abilities, including the Hawthorne Street Fair and the Portland Book Festival.

The Hawthorne District's involvement in and action for the community is another significant feature. The area has a long history of encouraging sustainable development and patronizing community businesses. For instance, the Hawthorne Boulevard Business Association promotes local economic growth and civic involvement through events like the Hawthorne Street Fair and the Hawthorne Hophouse Beer Festival.

Additionally, the Hawthorne District is home to a multicultural neighborhood that captures the distinct spirit of the area. Numerous other racial and socioeconomic groups, as well as a sizeable LGBTQ+ community, also reside in the area. The neighborhood's many community centers, including the Hawthorne Theatre, which presents a range of cultural activities and shows all year long, reflect this diversity.

The Hawthorne District has numerous advantages, but it also has some drawbacks. Concerns concerning the eviction of longtime inhabitants and the destruction of the neighborhood's cultural character have arisen as a result of rising housing costs and gentrification. Through programs like the Hawthorne Boulevard Alliance, which promotes affordable housing and equitable development in the neighborhood, the community is attempting to address these problems.

The Hawthorne District is an exceptional and dynamic area that highlights the finest of Portland's artistic, cultural, and civic participation. It serves as a role model for inclusive and equitable urban development due to its wide variety of stores, eateries, and community spaces, as well as its long history and dedication to sustainable development.

The Hawthorne District provides something for everyone, whether you're searching for a delicious lunch, a distinctive shopping experience, or an exciting cultural event.

Division Street Neighborhood

One of Portland, Oregon's most populated and vibrant areas is Division Street. From the Willamette River to Gresham, the street extends for more than 8 miles east to west. It is renowned for its energetic environment, diversified population, and extensive history. Division Street is a well-liked hangout for both locals and tourists because it is home to a variety of stores, eateries, pubs, and galleries.

Division Street has long served as Portland's center for commerce and transportation. The roadway was a section of the famed Oregon Trail in the early 20th century, which was essential to the US's westward migration. Early in the 20th century, Division Street served as a significant streetcar route connecting Sellwood and Richmond with downtown Portland.

Division Street is now a thriving and diverse neighborhood that captures Portland's evolving character. The area is noted for its creative energy and entrepreneurial attitude and is home to a mixture of longtime inhabitants and young professionals. Along the street, numerous small businesses have opened up shop, including independent shops, purveyors of artisanal food, and microbreweries.

The vibrant culinary scene on Division Street is one of its most recognized characteristics. The street is home to a wide variety of restaurants, from premium farm-to-table establishments to those serving traditional Vietnamese and Mexican dishes.

Ava Gene's, an Italian farm-to-table restaurant that has been named one of the best in the city by numerous publications, and Pok Pok, a Thai street food joint that has won national recognition for its bold flavors and inventive dishes, are two of the most well-known eateries on Division Street.

Division Street is renowned for its robust arts and entertainment sector in addition to its culinary offers. Numerous galleries and studios can be found on the street, including the renowned Littman Gallery, which exhibits the work of up-and-coming artists from all over the world. A number of cultural events are also held on Division Street throughout the year, such as the Division/Clinton Street Fair, which honors the various ethnic groups that live in the area.

Division Street has a lot to offer, but it also has its drawbacks. The inflow of young professionals has increased housing costs and forced some older residents out of the neighborhood, causing gentrification and affordability difficulties. To address these problems and guarantee that Division Street remains a thriving and diverse neighborhood for years to come, numerous locals and community organizations are working hard right now.

Division Street is a distinctive and vibrant neighborhood that depicts how Portland is evolving. Division Street is a must-visit location for anyone wanting to experience all that the city has to offer. This is because of its diverse population, thriving food scene, and extensive cultural activities. Division Street will undoubtedly continue to be a center for innovation and community for many years to come as Portland develops and grows.

CHAPTER 7

Portland day trips

The busy metropolis of Portland, Oregon is situated in the American Pacific Northwest. Portland is a popular travel destination for both domestic and foreign visitors because of its eccentric culture, delectable cuisine, and stunning natural surroundings.

Although there is no lack of sights and activities within the city limits, it can be enjoyable at times to travel outside the city limits and take in the local scenery. Fortunately, visitors can take a ton of day trips from Portland that offer a wide range of activities.

There is a day excursion from Portland to suit your interests, whether you're looking for outdoor adventure or a laid-back day spent sipping wine in the countryside. You may go hiking through lush forests, relax in natural hot springs, or see impressive waterfalls all within a short drive of the city. Additionally, you can visit quaint little towns, indulge in artisanal cheeses and chocolates, or go for a leisurely bike ride through vineyards. Additionally, you can even spend a day at the beach because the Pacific Ocean is only a few hours away.

You will be treated to breath-taking views and the chance to enjoy the particular beauty of the Pacific Northwest, regardless of the type of day excursion you select. When your adventure is over, you can come back to Portland and continue to take advantage of everything that this exciting city has to offer. So whether you enjoy the outdoors, good food, or just a change of scenery, think about including a day excursion from Portland on your itinerary; you won't be sorry.

Falls Multnomah

Multnomah Falls, one of the most well-liked natural attractions in the Pacific Northwest of the United States, is situated in the center of the Columbia River Gorge. Millions of people visit the waterfall each year because it is a magnificent sight to behold and is 620 feet tall. Being only 30 minutes away, Portland, Oregon is a great place to start a day trip to Multnomah Falls.

Driving through the Columbia River Gorge National Scenic Area on the way from Portland to Multnomah Falls is beautiful. With its 80-mile length, high cliffs, and luxuriant vegetation, this area provides some of the most breathtaking views of the Columbia River. There are many overlooks and viewing locations along the road, making it a terrific way to start your day excursion.

Columbia River Gorge

Portland, Oregon, is a buzzing metropolis with a booming food scene, hip cafes, and cultural attractions. The Columbia River Gorge, a natural marvel, is accessible to travelers by taking a short journey outside the city. This breath-taking valley, which hugs the Columbia River for more than 80 miles, is home to beautiful waterfalls, grand woods, and towering cliffs. A day excursion from Portland to Columbia River Gorge is the ideal opportunity to take in the region's natural splendor and get away from the bustle of the city.

Portland's downtown is only a 30-minute drive from the Columbia River Gorge, making it a great day trip location. Visitors can enjoy beautiful views of the river and the surrounding mountains as they travel along the historic Columbia River Highway. It is worthwhile to take the time to stop at any of the several overlooks along the route because the roadway was built in the early 1900s and is a National Historic Landmark.

Multnomah Falls, one of the most recognizable waterfalls in the area, should be one of the first stops on any day trip to the Columbia River Gorge. Visitors can get up close to the falls by ascending the paved trail to the Benson Bridge, which crosses the lower tier of them. This beautiful waterfall rushes down over 600 feet of steep cliff face. Visitors may admire the breathtaking gorge below from the bridge while also feeling the waterfall's mist.

Latourell Falls, another must-see waterfall in the Columbia River Gorge, is distinguished by its stunning columnar basalt formations. Visitors can go on a short stroll to get a closer look at the waterfall and the basalt cliffs that surround it.

This waterfall plunges more than 200 feet into a pool below. Bridal Veil Falls, Wahkeena Falls, and Horsetail Falls are just a few of the more waterfalls in the area, so tourists may easily spend an entire day exploring the many natural wonders of the Columbia River Gorge.

The Columbia River Gorge is home to several historical sites and tourist attractions in addition to waterfalls. The Bonneville Dam, which was constructed in the 1930s to supply hydroelectric power to the Pacific Northwest, is one of the most intriguing. The fish ladder, which permits salmon and other fish to avoid the dam and proceed upstream to their spawning grounds, can be explored by visitors who take a tour of the dam and learn about its construction and history.

The Vista House, which is built on a cliff above the river and provides breathtaking panoramic views of the gorge and the nearby mountains, is another notable location in the Columbia River Gorge. The Vista House is a museum and interpretive center that offers tourists a look into the history of the area. It was originally constructed in the early 1900s as a rest stop for motorists traveling along the Columbia River Highway.

The Columbia River Gorge provides many chances for hiking, biking, and other outdoor activities for those seeking a more active day excursion. Several state parks can be found in the gorge, such as the well-known Beacon Rock State Park, which offers a strenuous hike to the top of Beacon Rock, a massive basalt monolith that towers over 800 feet above the river.

Additionally, the region has a number of bike trails, such as the Historic Columbia River Highway State Trail, which is over 70 miles long and provides breathtaking views of the gorge and its numerous waterfalls.

Finally, a visit to one of the quaint communities that dot the area is a must on any day trip to the Columbia River Gorge. Hood River, one of the most well-liked, is well-known for its growing wine business as well as its numerous

Mount Hood

For any nature lover or outdoor enthusiast visiting Oregon, a day trip to Mount Hood is a must. The highest mountain in Oregon is Mount Hood, an active volcano that is situated in the Cascade Range. Due to the variety of activities it provides, including skiing, hiking, camping, and sightseeing, it is a well-liked vacation spot for both tourists and locals.

Around 60 miles separate Portland from Mount Hood in the time it takes to make the trip. The journey offers a fantastic introduction to the natural splendor of the Pacific Northwest as it passes through attractive landscapes, charming towns, and breathtaking woods.

The Mount Hood National Forest, which covers more than a million acres of pure wilderness, ought to be the first stop on the journey. The forest's extensive network of paths can be explored by visitors; these routes pass through lush forests, cross clear streams, and ascend to spectacular vistas.

The Timberline Trail, a 41-mile loop that around Mount Hood and provides breathtaking views of the volcano and the surroundings, is one of the most well-liked walks in the area. The Tom, Dick, and Harry Trail is a three-mile roundtrip climb that offers a breathtaking vantage point with views of the mountain and the nearby valley for those searching for a shorter hike.

Visitors can travel to the Timberline Lodge after exploring the forest, a historic mountain lodge that was constructed during the Great Depression and is now a National Historic Landmark. The lodge is a distinctive and charming destination because of its rustic architecture, hand-carved furniture, and local artwork.

The summit of Mount Hood, which offers amazing views of the Cascade Range and the surrounding landscape, is also accessible to visitors by a beautiful chairlift ride. The mountain also provides skiing and snowboarding during the winter for those seeking a more daring experience.

The Trillium Lake, a lovely lake not far from Mount Hood, is another well-liked stop on the journey. The lake is a well-liked location for fishing, kayaking, and picnicking and provides breathtaking views of the mountain.

The natural beauty and outdoor activities that Oregon has to offer may all be enjoyed on a day excursion from Portland to Mount Hood. Whether you prefer skiing, hiking, or simply taking in the scenery, Mount Hood has something to offer everyone. It is understandable why Mount Hood is regarded as one of the top tourist destinations in the Pacific Northwest with its breathtaking landscape, fascinating history, and variety of activities.

Willamette Valley Wine Country

In Oregon, the Willamette Valley is renowned for its beautiful scenery, undulating hills, and top-notch wines. The Willamette Valley Wine Country is a must-visit location for wine enthusiasts and anybody who appreciates the natural beauty of the Pacific Northwest, and it's only a short drive from Portland.

The best vineyards and wineries in the area can be visited in a day trip from Portland to the Willamette Valley Wine Country. An easy and practical day excursion, it takes around an hour to get from Portland to the Willamette Valley.

Taking a tour is among the greatest ways to discover the Willamette Valley Wine Country. A number of tour companies provide led excursions around the area that take guests to some of the top wineries and vineyards. These excursions are a fantastic way to discover the history of winemaking in the area and the distinctive terroir that makes the Willamette Valley such a unique location for wine production.

Visitors also have the option to self-drive and plan their own routes. Wineries including Archery Summit, Adelsheim Vineyard, Domaine Serene, and Stoller Family Estate are among the most well-liked places to visit. Each winery has its own distinct style, using various grape varietals and winemaking methods.

Many of the wineries offer tours and tastings for guests seeking a more in-depth experience. A walk through the vineyards, education about the wine-making process, and tasting some of the best wines the area has to offer are frequently included in these trips. With breathtaking views of the valley and the surrounding countryside, the vineyards themselves are also worthwhile exploring.

The Willamette Valley Wine Country provides a variety of culinary activities in addition to wine sampling. Numerous wineries have their own eateries, providing a farm-to-table dining experience that highlights the best produce from the area. The finest wines the area has to offer can be coupled with a leisurely lunch or dinner for visitors.

The Willamette Valley also provides a variety of outdoor activities for those searching for a more active experience. Through the valley, there are numerous hiking and biking trails that provide breathtaking views of the surrounding countryside. Additionally, a number of hot air balloon companies provide scenic flights over the valley, offering a distinctive viewpoint of the area.

The Willamette Valley Wine Country can be reached by day trip from Portland and is a wonderful place to see Oregon's natural beauty and delectable cuisine. The Willamette Valley has something for everyone, whether you decide to go on a guided trip or design your own schedule. The Willamette Valley offers everything from top-notch wines to farm-to-table cuisine and outdoor excursions.

CHAPTER 8

Portland's Restaurants and Bars

Portland, Oregon is known for having a thriving restaurant, bar, cafe, and brewery sector that offers something for every taste and price range. Portland, which located in the Pacific Northwest, is a center for culinary innovation, drawing its inspiration from regional foods, global cuisines, and a dedication to sustainability and community.

Portland provides several options to please your palate and sate your appetites, whether you're a foodie, a beer enthusiast, or simply looking to discover the city's distinct culture and cuisine.

The emphasis on locally produced, seasonal, and organic ingredients is one of Portland's food and drink scene's distinguishing traits. Portlanders take pride in supporting small-scale producers and sustainable agriculture, which has led to a lively and constantly evolving culinary scene, including farm-to-table restaurants and farmers' markets. Fresh seafood and wine are abundant in the city because of its close proximity to the Pacific Ocean, the Willamette Valley wine region, and the Cascade Mountains.

Portland's Restaurant Scene

The city of Portland, Oregon is known as a haven for foodies. Everything from vegan doughnuts to fresh seafood can be found in abundance in the city's renowned diverse and creative food scene. Portland has developed into a center for some of the most exciting and delectable food in the United States thanks to a focus on using locally sourced, sustainably grown products and a strong emphasis on creativity and experimentation.

Portland is distinguished by, among other things, its profusion of food carts. These portable restaurants can be found all around the city and offer everything from traditional American burgers to Korean fusion food. Portland boasts one of the highest concentrations of street food in the world, with over 500 food carts dispersed across the city. These carts are well-liked by both locals and tourists since they provide a quick and inexpensive opportunity to experience a variety of cuisines.

In addition to having a robust restaurant industry, Portland also has food carts. Many of the city's restaurants and award-winning chefs are committed to using locally sourced and sustainably grown ingredients. National recognition has been bestowed upon eateries like Ava Gene's, Le Pigeon, and Paley's Place for their creative menus and dedication to employing the freshest seasonal ingredients. There are many great restaurants in Portland, from premium fine dining spots to farm-to-table bistros.

The emphasis on vegetarian and vegan cuisine in Portland's food scene is another distinctive feature. With its abundance of vegetarian and vegan eateries, food carts, and cafes, the city has long been a popular destination for those seeking plant-based cuisine. Due to their creative and flavorful menus, well-known restaurants like Blossoming Lotus, Farm Spirit, and Back to Eden Bakery are adored by both vegetarians and meat eaters.

Seafood enthusiasts will find Portland to be the perfect vacation spot because of its proximity to the Pacific Ocean. Fresh oysters, crab, and salmon are particularly well-liked local seafood dishes that are common in Portland eateries. Restaurants like Eventide Oyster Co., Roe, and Jacqueline have drawn notice from throughout the country for their seafood-heavy menus that highlight the best of coastal cuisine from the Pacific Northwest.

The emphasis on community and collaboration in Portland's food sector is one of its defining characteristics. In order to obtain products and support regional farmers and producers, many restaurants and food carts collaborate.

The city also holds a variety of food-related festivals and events throughout the year, such as the Vegan Beer and Food Festival, Feast Portland, and the Portland Farmers Market. Chefs, farmers, and food enthusiasts from all around the area get together at these events to celebrate Portland's thriving culinary scene.

Overall, the city's forward-thinking, creative ethos is reflected in Portland's cuisine sector.

Cafes and coffee shops

The robust coffee and cafe scene in Portland, Oregon is well-known. There are countless coffee shops and cafes in the city, each with an own atmosphere, menu, and devoted clientele. The coffee and café scene in Portland will be examined in this essay, along with its history, present situation, and potential future.

Portland has a lengthy history with coffee culture that dates back to the early 1900s. Small neighborhood shops were used to roast and brew coffee at the time, and coffeehouses served as community hubs where people gathered to socialize, discuss politics, and enjoy the arts and literature.

In the 1960s, Portland experienced the arrival of the first espresso machine, which ushered in a new era of coffee culture. Coffee shops started to open up and started providing lattes, cappuccinos, and regular drip coffee.

Portland now has one of the strongest coffee cultures in the country.

Portland's coffee culture is distinctive in part because it places a strong premium on locally roasted and sourced beans. In Portland, there are lots of coffee cafes with their own roasting facilities where they roast their own beans to make unique blends and flavors. Because of the focus on local sourcing, there is now a culture of cooperation between local farmers and coffee shops, which has made the coffee industry more ethical and sustainable.

Coffee houses and cafés in Portland are renowned for their unique and varied offerings. Many coffee shops also serve tea, smoothies, pastries, sandwiches, and other snacks in addition to coffee. Portland's populace is socially and health-conscious, thus there are lots of vegan and gluten-free options available. Portland's dedication to ethical and ecological food practices is further highlighted by the city's cafes, which frequently serve seasonal and local cuisine.

The social and cultural fabric of Portland is significantly influenced by the coffee and café culture. Coffee shops serve as meeting spaces for individuals of different ages and socioeconomic backgrounds, offering a setting for interaction, community development, and conversation.

The fact that so many coffee shops and cafes hold activities like poetry readings, book clubs, and live music enhances their status as cultural centers. Additionally, Portland's thriving art scene and coffee and cafe culture are frequently intertwined, with many coffee shops hosting local artists' installations and exhibitions.

The COVID-19 pandemic has presented obstacles, but Portland's coffee and cafe scene has persevered. With the advent of online ordering, delivery, and outside sitting, many coffee shops and cafés adjusted. Additionally, a lot of stores and cafes have taken advantage of the pandemic to innovate, creating new menu items and putting in place new business models that enable them to survive in a changing environment.

Portland's coffee and cafe sector appears to be well-positioned for long-term expansion and innovation. Portland's coffee is known for its emphasis on ethical and environmental processes, dedication to local sourcing, and commitment to fostering community.

Distilleries and Breweries

B reweries and distilleries are places where alcoholic drinks including beer, wine, spirits, and liqueurs are made. These organizations have existed for many years and have had a big impact on the development of the global economy and culture. In this paper, we'll look at the development and history of breweries and distilleries, as well as their social effects and potential.

Breweries and distilleries have existed for thousands of years. According to archaeological findings, ancient Egyptians, Greeks, and Romans all produced beer or wine in some capacity. The earliest methods for making these drinks were primitive and entailed fermenting grains or fruit in clay or wood containers. But as technology developed, so did the processes used to make these drinks. Breweries and distilleries had advanced by the Middle Ages, and the quality of the alcoholic beverages they produced had substantially increased.

Breweries and distilleries have contributed significantly to the development of global culture over the years. While spirits and liqueurs have been used for medicinal purposes and as a source of inspiration for artists and writers, beer and wine have long been a staple of many social and religious gatherings. For instance, during the American Prohibition era, numerous well-known authors and painters, including Ernest Hemingway and F. Scott Fitzgerald and others were inspired by the culture and ambiance of speakeasies and attended them.

Breweries and distilleries still play a big role in the world economy today. The global market for alcoholic drinks was estimated to be worth $1.36 trillion in 2019 and is projected to grow to $1.64 trillion by 2027, according to a survey by Allied Market Research. This industry is expanding as a result of rising disposable income, shifting consumer tastes, and the growing appeal of craft beer and artisanal spirits.

The growth of craft breweries and distilleries is one of the most important trends in the sector right now. Small-batch, artisanal beverages are frequently created by these businesses utilizing conventional techniques and regional ingredients.

More than 8,000 craft brewers are already operating in the United States alone, and the craft beer industry in particular has experienced phenomenal expansion in recent years. Consumers' demand for distinctive, high-quality goods that are representative of their values and interests has fueled this trend.

Breweries and distilleries encounter a number of difficulties despite the development of the sector. The industry's increased regulation is one of the biggest obstacles. The manufacturing and marketing of alcoholic beverages are subject to increasing regulations from governments all over the world, which can drive up costs and stifle innovation. Additionally, other beverages like non-alcoholic beer and spirits and drinks with a focus on health pose a significant threat to the industry.

The world economy and culture are significantly influenced by breweries and distilleries. These institutions have existed for many centuries and have had a significant impact on world history and culture. Despite the new challenges the sector is currently facing, such as increased regulation and competition, it is still a thriving and dynamic sector with significant growth potential.

Breweries and distilleries are well-positioned to meet the need for distinctive and high-quality products from customers, and they will remain a prominent influence in the global economy.

Pods and carts for food

With an array of eateries, cafes, and food carts dotted across the city, Portland, Oregon, is renowned for its thriving food culture.

However, in recent years, food carts and food pods have experienced a meteoric rise in popularity, becoming an essential part of the city's culinary scene.

Mobile food sellers, commonly referred to as food trucks or food carts, set up shop in specific locations across the city. These carts provide food from all over the world, including Korean BBQ and Thai noodles as well as classic American fare like burgers and fries. Many of them have a devoted following of devoted customers who seek out their distinctive flavors and inventive dishes. They typically operate out of a small truck or trailer.

On the other hand, food pods are fixed clusters of food carts that are placed in a certain location. These pods frequently contain communal seating spaces and offer patrons a stimulating and energetic environment in which to enjoy their meals. They can be found all over Portland, from the city center to more suburban areas, and each pod has a distinctive personality and menu to offer.

The accessibility of food carts and food pods is one of the reasons why Portlanders have grown to love them. A lot of these sellers sell tasty, high-quality cuisine for a lot less than you would pay at a regular restaurant. This makes them a desirable choice for residents and guests searching for a delicious supper at a reasonable price.

Their emphasis on sustainability and local sourcing is another factor in their popularity. The use of fresh, locally sourced foods and eco-friendly packaging is prioritized by many food cart and pod merchants. Due to its dedication to sustainability, Portland has become a national leader in the food cart movement and is known as a center for cutting-edge, environmentally friendly cuisine.

Additionally, food carts and pods offer a distinctive chance for small business owners and entrepreneurs to launch their own culinary businesses. A food cart or pod is an affordable solution for those who do not have the funds to launch a conventional brick-and-mortar restaurant because to its minimal startup expenses. As a result, Portland boasts a thriving and diverse community of food vendors, with a large number of these establishments being run by women and people of color.

Last but not least, food trucks and pods create a lively scene for guests to enjoy. The fact that many of these vendors are situated outside enables guests to take advantage of the city's pleasant climate and tour other areas while savoring a delectable lunch. Additionally, the communal seating areas at food pods offer a special chance to network and socialize while enjoying delicious food.

In conclusion, Portland's culinary scene has benefited greatly from the growth of food carts and food pods, which provide a wide variety of inexpensive and sustainable cuisine in addition to promoting a dynamic and welcoming community of small business owners and entrepreneurs. A food cart or pod experience is a must-try when experiencing the city's culinary delights, whether you're a local or a guest.

Farmers' markets

Farmers' markets have gained popularity in recent years in places all around the United States, and Portland, Oregon is no exception. Portland is renowned for its food scene and focus on sustainability, making it a perfect place for farmers and producers to market and sell their locally produced goods.

Local farmers and producers join together at a farmer's market to offer their wares to the public. During the warmer months, these markets are typically held weekly and take place in open areas like parks, parking lots, or streets. They give customers the chance to buy fresh, regional food and other goods directly from the grower or producer, frequently at a lesser price than in supermarkets.

Portland's emphasis on sustainability and supporting local companies is one of the reasons farmer's markets have grown so popular there. Residents can lessen their carbon footprint by limiting the distance their food travels from farm to table by supporting local farms and producers.

Additionally, patronizing nearby establishments helps the neighborhood's economic development by keeping money there.

The high quality of the goods sold at Portland's farmer's markets is another factor in their rising popularity. Produce that is better-tasting and more nutrient-dense is produced because local farmers and producers are able to harvest and sell their goods at the height of their freshness. Additionally, a lot of these farmers and producers employ organic and sustainable farming methods, so the food is free of dangerous pesticides and chemicals.

There are numerous farmer's markets spread out over Portland, each having an own personality and selection of goods. The largest and most established market in the city, the Portland Farmers Market, is held every Saturday in the South Park Blocks from March through December. More than 200 merchants provide a variety of things at this market, including baked foods, artisanal crafts, and fresh produce.

Another well-known market in Portland is the Hollywood Farmers Market, which is open every Saturday from May through October. This market, which has more than 50 sellers, is renowned for the wide variety of vegetables and locally created goods it offers.

These markets offer a variety of items and services, including food and beverages, as well as community events and activities. For instance, the Portland Farmers Market offers cooking classes, live entertainment, and kid- and adult-friendly educational seminars. These gatherings foster a sense of neighborhood and unite individuals around a love of food and sustainability.

The competition from bigger grocery shops and online sellers is one of the difficulties that farmer's markets encounter. However, a lot of people are willing to spend more money on locally produced food and handcrafted goods because they frequently have a higher quality and more distinctive appeal.

A more intimate and interesting shopping experience is also provided through farmer's markets, where shoppers may talk to the farmers and producers and discover more about the goods they are buying.

CHAPTER 9

Practical Information

The largest city in Oregon, Portland, is a bustling, diverse tourist attraction that draws people from all over the world. Portland, a city in the Pacific Northwest of the United States, is renowned for its picturesque landscape, thriving arts and cultural scene, and distinctive neighborhoods. Everyone can find something to do in Portland, from outdoor excursions to gastronomic highlights.

We will go over everything you need to know to prepare the ideal vacation to Portland in this useful informational guide. We will discuss the top areas, eateries, and activities in the city as well as offer advice on getting around, finding lodging, and setting a budget.

Whether you've been to Portland before or not, our guide will help you get the most out of your trip. You'll discover information about the city's well-known parks, remarkable art and museum scene, and its numerous and delectable dining options. We'll guide you through the most fascinating districts of the city, highlighting the must-see attractions along the route, from the hipster refuge of the Pearl District to the trendy Alberta Arts District.

In order to make it easier for you to move around the city, we'll also show you how to use Portland's large light rail network, streetcars, and buses. In addition, we'll offer suggestions for hotels, hostels, and vacation rentals in a range of pricing ranges if you're seeking for advice on where to stay.

Portland is a city that values uniqueness and originality, and we hope that our guide will motivate you to take advantage of all that this exciting place has to offer. Pack your luggage, grab your hiking boots, and get ready to discover Portland at its best.

Safety and health

P rioritizing health and safety is vital while making travel plans to Portland. There are many actions you can take to guarantee a secure and healthy journey, from drinking plenty of water to covering up from the sun.

Water consumption is one of the most crucial things to remember when in Portland. Although the city is renowned for its mild, rainy climate, summertime temperatures can rise quickly. When you're out and about exploring the city, it's simple to become dehydrated, so bring a reusable water bottle and fill it up at one of the many public fountains or hydration stations located all over the place.

Avoiding the sun is a crucial part of maintaining your health while traveling. Even though Portland isn't known for its sunny days, it's still important to wear sunscreen and protective clothing. Apply a broad-spectrum sunscreen with an SPF of at least 30 and wear a hat and sunglasses to protect your skin from the sun's harmful rays, which can still reach your skin through clouds and cause skin damage.

Portland is a culinary hotspot with a thriving food culture, but it's crucial to be aware of food safety. Always wash your hands, especially before handling or eating food. Check to see if the food cart or outside restaurant has a high sanitary rating from the health department before you eat there.

It's crucial to be aware of any potential allergies in the foods you eat in addition to food safety. While many Portland restaurants and food carts provide allergen-free options, it's always a good idea to enquire about the ingredients and let the establishment know if you have any dietary restrictions or allergies.

Light rail, streetcars, and buses are just a few of the alternatives Portland residents have for getting about. Although these choices are practical and environmentally friendly, it's crucial to use caution when traveling by public transportation. Be mindful of your surroundings, particularly at night or in strange places. Keep your possessions close to hand and watch out for pickpockets and other potential security risks.

Finally, it's critical to be ready for any potential emergency situations. As well as packing any necessary prescriptions or medical supplies, be sure your travel insurance covers medical emergencies. Know where the closest hospitals or urgent care facilities are located, and have a plan in place in case of an emergency.

Portland is a friendly city with lots of chances for exploration and adventure. By putting your health and safety first, you can fully take advantage of everything that this energetic city has to offer.

Emergency Information

It's crucial to be ready for emergencies when visiting a new place. Although Portland is a friendly and safe city, unforeseen circumstances can still occur. An informed and well-planned journey is something you can guarantee.

The first thing you should do before your trip is research Portland's emergency services. This involves being aware of the phone numbers for the police, fire, and ambulance as well as other emergency services. The emergency phone number in the US is 911. In case of a medical emergency, it's also critical to know where the closest hospitals and urgent care facilities are.

Make sure you have travel insurance that covers medical crises, trip cancellation, and other unforeseen situations as another method to be prepared for emergencies. Knowing that you are protected in case of an emergency will provide you comfort.

It's a good idea to become familiar with Portland's layout and transit alternatives before you visit. This entails knowing the locations of neighboring taxi ranks or ridesharing services as well as knowing how to use public transportation, such as the light rail and buses. In an emergency, being able to move swiftly and effectively around the city can be essential.

In the event of a natural disaster, such as an earthquake or severe weather occurrence, it is also critical to have a plan in place. Knowing what to do in the event of an earthquake is crucial because Portland is situated in an earthquake-prone area. This includes having a supply of food, water, and other necessary supplies in case of a prolonged power outage or evacuation, as well as finding a secure hiding location, such as behind a doorway or beneath a substantial piece of furniture.

In case of an emergency, it's a good idea to have a communication strategy in place. This includes choosing a location for your group's gathering and ensuring that everyone has a phone or walkie-talkie they can use to communicate. In the event of a serious emergency, it's a good idea to have a strategy in place for calling family members back home to let them know you are safe.

Every trip requires some level of emergency planning, and Portland is no exception. Your vacation to Portland can be safe and successful if you do your research on local emergency services, have travel insurance, are familiar with the city's layout and transit options, have a plan in place for natural disasters, and have a communication plan in place.

Sustainable Travel Advice

Portland, Oregon is a thriving and environmentally conscious city renowned for its green lifestyle, cutting-edge transportation options, and dedication to environmental preservation. There are several environmentally friendly travel choices available to city visitors, including eco-friendly hotels, public transit, and regional food and drink. We'll look at some advice for environmentally friendly travel to Portland in this essay.

First, think about booking a green hotel. From boutique bed & breakfasts that place an emphasis on sustainability to LEED-certified hotels, Portland offers a variety of environmentally friendly housing options. The Jupiter Hotel in Portland, which uses sustainable materials and has a rooftop garden, and the Kimpton Hotel Monaco, which gives visitors free bicycles to use while exploring the city, are two famous eco-friendly hotels.

Utilizing Portland's extensive public transportation network is an additional sustainable mode of transportation. Numerous of the city's most well-known attractions can be reached by visitors using the bus, light rail, and streetcar services provided by TriMet, the local transportation agency. Additionally, BIKETOWN, the city's bike share program, gives visitors an inexpensive and sustainable way to tour the city on two wheels.

Portland is renowned for its farm-to-table cuisine and variety of locally produced food and drink options when it comes to dining. By dining at establishments that emphasize locally sourced ingredients and sustainable processes, patrons can support sustainable agriculture. Ava Gene's, which obtains its products from regional farmers and producers, and Farm Spirit, a plant-based eatery that uses sustainable methods including composting and little waste, are two famous sustainable restaurants in Portland.

Visitors to Portland can contribute to sustainable tourism in addition to eating sustainably by choosing to engage in environmentally friendly activities. The city has a range of outdoor recreation options, including kayaking on the Willamette River and hiking at Forest Park. The city's numerous parks and gardens, such as the Portland Japanese Garden and the International Rose Test Garden, which both emphasize sustainable gardening techniques, are also open to visitors.

Supporting regional companies and craftspeople is another option to travel responsibly in Portland. Visitors can buy locally created goods and support small businesses by shopping at the city's numerous farmers' markets and artisan fairs. Visitors can also support sustainable fashion by making purchases at neighborhood stores like Nisolo and Altar PDX that emphasize ethical and environmentally friendly apparel processes.

Finally, by engaging in eco-friendly behaviors while they are in Portland, travelers can lessen their influence on the environment. This can involve taking public transportation, walking or bicycling instead of driving, using reusable coffee and water bottles, and properly disposing of trash in recycling and compost bins.

Visitors may also decide to participate in a carbon offset scheme, such as those run by some airlines or by businesses like Carbonfund.org, in order to reduce their carbon footprints.

Portland provides a variety of environmentally friendly travel choices that let visitors explore the city while reducing their influence on the environment. Visitors can have a pleasurable and sustainable vacation experience in this dynamic and forward-thinking city by picking eco-friendly lodging, taking the bus and biking, eating at sustainable restaurants, buying local goods and supporting local craftsmen.

Exchange of money and currencies

Portland, a thriving city in the Pacific Northwest of the United States, with a broad economy and a thriving tourism sector. Portland serves as a global hub for business and pleasure, and a key component of the city's financial infrastructure is currency exchange. The many types of currencies that are accepted, the exchange rates, and the various methods of exchanging money in the city of Portland will all be covered in this essay.

Currencies accepted in Portland

Portland, like the rest of the nation, uses the United States Dollar (USD) as its main form of payment. However, a lot of establishments in Portland also take other money, including the Euro (EUR) and the Canadian dollar (CAD). This is especially true for establishments that serve travelers, like hotels, eateries, and gift shops. These currencies may have different exchange rates depending on the market rate at the time, although they are typically accepted at a rate that is close to the current rate.

Portland's exchange rates for currency

Like in any other city, Portland's foreign exchange rates fluctuate according to the currency being exchanged and the going market rate. The amount of one currency that can be exchanged for another is known as the exchange rate, and it continually changes depending on many economic conditions. Major currencies like the Euro or the Canadian dollar will typically have better exchange rates than less popular currencies.

It's crucial to remember that the exchange rate may not be precisely the same as the current market rate while converting money in Portland. The way money exchange firms normally generate their profit is by marking up the exchange rate. Before exchanging money, it is a good idea to shop around and compare rates since some providers might offer more enticing terms than others.

Money Exchange Options in Portland

In Portland, there are several possibilities for exchanging money, from conventional banks and currency exchange companies to online options.

Banks: The majority of Portland's big banks provide currency exchange services, albeit their fees could be more expensive than those of specialized companies. Typically, in order to exchange currency, banks demand that their clients have an account with them.

Providers of Foreign Currency Exchange: Portland is home to a number of providers of foreign currency exchange. These companies frequently provide better conversion rates than banks and could have a wider selection of available currencies.

Online currency exchange: There are various online currency exchange companies that allow consumers to exchange currencies from their computer or mobile device, which is convenient for individuals who like online banking. Since they do not have the overhead expenses associated with physical locations, online providers might provide more favorable exchange rates than traditional providers.

ATMs: Using an ATM is another alternative for converting money in Portland. However, there may be charges associated with using an ATM to withdraw money in a foreign currency, such as foreign transaction fees and ATM fees.

Portland is a welcoming city that offers a broad financial infrastructure to meet the needs of its tourists from all over the world. The city has a number of ways to exchange currencies and accepts a number of foreign currencies, including the Canadian, American, and European currencies. It's crucial to browse around and compare rates when changing money in Portland in order to get the greatest value.

Visitors can thus take pleasure in their time in Portland without worrying about money exchange by doing this.

Language

Portland, a city in the Pacific Northwest of the United States, is home to a wide variety of languages. Portland's language is influenced by a variety of historical factors, cultural diversity, and the city's distinct personality. We will look at the several languages spoken in Portland, their historical and cultural effects, and how language reflects the character of the city in this essay.

Spoken Languages in Portland

English, the official language of the United States, is the major language used in Portland. However, many other languages are also spoken in Portland as a result of the city's diverse population. Among the many languages used in Portland are Spanish, Mandarin Chinese, Vietnamese, Russian, and Somali. Furthermore, Portland has a thriving

American Sign Language (ASL) community with a large number of native ASL speakers.

Language in Portland Has Been Influenced by History and Culture

There are many different influences that have impacted Portland's history and language. Native American groups such the Chinook, Kalapuya, and Multnomah people historically called the city home. Due to colonization and cultural assimilation, several of these tribes once spoke their own distinctive languages and dialects, which have since virtually disappeared.

However, the names of famous landmarks and locations in and around Portland, such as the Columbia River, which was given that name in honor of the Columbia tribe, still reflect the influence of these languages.

Portland experienced an influx of immigrants from Europe and Asia in the 19th century who brought their own languages and customs. The languages of their native nations, German, Italian, and Scandinavian, were widely spoken by immigrants. Along with their own Mandarin and Cantonese dialects, Chinese immigrants also arrived in Portland in large numbers to work in the railroads and other industries.

Portland's language now is influenced by the city's diverse population, which includes sizable Hispanic and Asian populations. Spanish is the second most often spoken language in Portland, and many locals are bilingual in the two languages. Mandarin and Cantonese are two languages that are commonly spoken in Portland, where the Chinese minority has continued to have a strong cultural influence.

Language and the Identity of Portland

Portland's distinctive identity as a progressive, welcoming, and culturally diverse city is reflected in its language. Portland is known for being a kind and accommodating city, and this is reflected in the language. The city's dedication to cultural diversity and inclusivity is demonstrated by the variety of languages that are spoken there.

Portland's progressive politics and social activities are also reflected in the language of the city. In Portland, inclusive language is frequently used, which demonstrates the city's dedication to social justice and equality. Examples include the use of gender-neutral pronouns and terminology.

Portland's language is a reflection of the city's rich history, numerous cultural influences, and distinctive personality. even if English is the main tongue

Useful Phrases

Portland is a vibrant and a beautiful city located in the Pacific Northwest region of the United States. It is known for its lively music and arts scene, outdoor recreation opportunities, and its eco-friendly and sustainable ethos. If you plan on visiting Portland, it's important to familiarize yourself with some useful phrases that will help you navigate the city with ease.

"Keep Portland Weird"

This phrase is a motto of sorts for the city, and it refers to Portland's unique and eclectic culture. It encourages people to embrace their quirks and individuality, and to celebrate the offbeat and unconventional aspects of the city.

"Where's the MAX?"

The MAX is Portland's light rail system, which connects various neighborhoods and suburbs throughout the city. If you need to get somewhere quickly, asking someone where the nearest MAX station is can be very helpful.

"I'll have a Voodoo doughnut, please"

Voodoo Doughnut is a famous doughnut shop in Portland that is known for its creative and unique flavors. If you have a sweet tooth, be sure to stop by and try one of their signature doughnuts.

"Is there a food cart pod nearby?"

Portland is home to hundreds of food carts that serve a wide range of cuisines, from Thai to Mexican to vegan. If you're hungry and looking for a quick and delicious meal, asking someone where the nearest food cart pod is can lead you to some of the best eats in the city.

"Do you have any recommendations for a nice brewery?"

Portland is known for its craft beer scene, and there are dozens of breweries and taprooms scattered throughout the city. If you're a beer lover, asking someone for their favorite brewery recommendation can lead you to some tasty and unique brews.

"What's the weather like today?"

Portland is known for its rainy and mild weather, so it's always a good idea to check the forecast before heading out for the day. Asking someone about the weather can help you plan your activities and ensure that you're dressed appropriately.

"Excuse me, could you help me find my way to (insert destination here)?"

Portland is a relatively easy city to navigate, but it's always helpful to ask for directions if you're unfamiliar with the area. Portlanders are generally friendly and welcoming, and most people will be happy to help you find your way.

"What's your favorite hike in the area?"
Portland is surrounded by stunning natural beauty, including the Columbia River Gorge and Mount Hood. If you're looking to get some fresh air and exercise, asking someone for their favorite hiking spot can lead you to some breathtaking vistas and scenic trails.

Portland is a vibrant and unique city that is well worth a visit. By familiarizing yourself with these useful phrases, you'll be able to navigate the city with ease and make the most of your time there. Whether you're exploring the food cart scene, sipping craft beer, or hiking through the great outdoors, Portland has something to offer everyone.

Local customs and etiquette

P ortland, Oregon, is a city known for its friendly and laid-back culture. The locals take pride in their city and value respect for their customs and etiquette. Whether you're visiting or moving to Portland, it's essential to be aware of the local customs and etiquette to avoid any misunderstandings and show respect for the community.

One of the most important things to know about Portland is that it is a very environmentally conscious city. It is known for its recycling and composting programs, and the locals take great pride in keeping the city clean and green. As a visitor or resident, it's important to do your part in maintaining this culture by using the recycling and composting bins available and avoiding littering.

The importance placed on locally sourced and sustainable food is another significant component of Portland's culture. The city is home to many eateries that place a strong emphasis on employing local ingredients. In Portland, it's typical to see menu dishes that emphasize the places where the food came from. Additionally, tipping is accepted and the customary amount is 20% of the final bill.

Portland is renowned for its distinctive sense of fashion and flair. In this city, where originality is highly valued, it's common to see people expressing themselves through their attire and accessories. People with unusual clothing or hair colors are commonplace. However, it's crucial to respect others' personal space and refrain from touching or making comments about someone's appearance without their consent.

Portland has a vibrant biking community, and many commuters opt to ride bikes rather than use their cars. It's crucial to be mindful of bike lanes and share the road with cyclists as a result. Additionally, it is customary to wait for pedestrians to cross the street before turning and to yield to them at crosswalks.

Portland is a city that respects diversity and upholds inclusivity. Discrimination based on gender, ethnicity, or sexual orientation is not tolerated, and rainbow flags and other LGBTQ+ pride symbols may be seen all around the city. Use people's preferred pronouns and refrain from assuming anything about their sexual orientation or gender identity.

Finally, when attending events or gatherings in Portland, it's critical to understand the customs and etiquette of the area. It is expected that you will arrive on time or a few minutes early, and it is disrespectful to be late without a good reason. Furthermore, it's crucial to respect others' personal space and refrain from approaching them too closely or touching them without their consent.

Both visitors and locals must be aware of and respectful of the regional customs and manners in Portland. By doing this, you can prevent misunderstandings, respect the neighborhood, and fully appreciate this bustling city's distinctive culture. Portland has a lot to offer, from ecology to inclusivity, and by adhering to these rules, you may fully immerse yourself in the city's rich cultural past.

CONCLUSION

Portland, Oregon, is a lively, diverse city with a distinctive culture that attracts tourists from all over the world. Portland has much to offer everyone, from its breathtaking natural settings to its bustling arts scene.

As a result, it has recently gained popularity as a travel destination. We've discussed some of Portland's best sights and things to do in our travel guide, as well as details on the history and culture of the area.

Portland's scenic surroundings are one of its key attractions. The city is encircled by breathtaking forests, rivers, and waterfalls and is located in the shadow of Mount Hood. The Columbia River Gorge, which offers hiking trails, beautiful drives, and spectacular views, is one of the most well-known natural attractions in the region.

The International Rose Test Garden, which has over 10,000 roses in over 650 kinds, is another must-visit location. It's a wonderful location for a leisurely stroll while seeing the lovely flowers.

Portland is renowned for having a robust arts and cultural community. The Portland Art Museum, the Museum of Contemporary Craft, and the Oregon Historical Society are just a few of the city's many museums and galleries.

Portland has a thriving live music culture, with venues ranging from tiny, intimate clubs to huge arenas. Additionally, the city is home to several theater companies that present a variety of productions, from traditional plays to avant-garde works.

Portland offers a lot to foodies as well. With a wide variety of eateries and food carts serving everything from traditional American fare to international cuisine, the city boasts a flourishing food culture. Over 100 breweries make up Portland's thriving craft beer scene, which is especially well-known. A strong coffee culture with a wide variety of independent coffee shops and roasters is also present there.

Portland's progressive and ecologically sensitive culture is one of its most distinctive features. With a robust public transportation network, bike-friendly streets, and a focus on organic, locally sourced food, the city is strongly committed to sustainability. Portland is renowned for its eccentric and varied atmosphere, strong music and art scenes, and distinctive sense of style.

The city of Portland has a lot to offer. Portland offers something for everyone, from its breathtaking natural surroundings to its vibrant arts and entertainment scene. Portland is unquestionably worth a visit, whether you are a fan of the outdoors, fine dining, live music, or simply want to see a distinctive and energetic city.

Portland is a city that is likely to make an impression on everybody who visits because to its dedication to sustainability and its eccentric and eclectic culture.

Recommendation

In recent years, Portland, Oregon, has grown in popularity as a tourism destination because of its distinctive culture, vibrant food scene, and stunning natural surroundings. As a large language model, I have access to a wealth of knowledge and am able to provide a thorough Portland travel guide with suggestions for things to do, restaurants to visit, and lodging options.

Actions to Take: Discover Forest Park: One of the largest urban parks in the nation, Forest Park has over 5,000 acres of lush forest and trails. There are numerous hiking and biking paths available, in addition to picnic sites and breathtaking vistas.

Visit the Portland Japanese Garden: This tranquil haven in the middle of the city is called the Portland Japanese Garden. It has peaceful gardens, soothing water features, and traditional Japanese buildings.

Visit the Portland Art Museum: It houses a sizable collection of works of art from all over the world and is the oldest art museum in the Pacific Northwest. Additionally, it hosts unique exhibitions and occasions all year long.

Explore Powell's City of Books: It has over a million books to choose from and is the biggest independent bookstore in the world. For book fans, it's a must-go, and even those who aren't avid readers will enjoy the store's distinctive ambience.

Visit the Oregon Museum of Science and Industry (OMSI): This interactive science museum is enjoyable for visitors of all ages. It has an IMAX theater, a planetarium, and interactive displays.

Where to Eat: Pok Pok: Pok Pok is a well-known Thai eatery known for its wings and other traditional fare. Although there are several locations throughout the city, you should definitely go to the original one on Southeast Division Street.

Local ice cream parlor Salt & Straw serves unusual tastes like honey lavender and sea salt with caramel ribbons. Even though there may be lengthy queues, it's worth it.

Cast iron frittatas and smoked brisket hash are just a couple of the substantial brunch fare that Tasty n Alder serves. It's a nice place for a brunch on the weekends.

Blue Star Donuts: Blue Star Donuts is a gourmet doughnut shop with distinctive flavors including Meyer lemon and key lime curd and blueberry bourbon basil. They cost a little more than the typical donut, but the quality is worthwhile.

Andina: The Peruvian restaurant Andina serves a wide range of food, including ceviche and grilled meats. The ambiance of the restaurant is cozy and welcoming, and the food is consistently excellent.

The Nines: In the center of Portland's business district is a luxurious hotel called The Nines. In addition to modern accommodations, a rooftop bar, and a fitness center, it is built in a historical structure.

Ace Hotel: Situated in the Pearl District, the Ace Hotel is a hip hotel. It has distinctive rooms decorated in an industrial design, a well-liked coffee shop, and a busy bar.

Hotel Monaco: In the heart of Portland, there is a boutique hotel called the Hotel Monaco. It has upscale accommodations, a daily wine hour, and a pet-friendly setting.

McMenamins Kennedy School: Located in a former primary school, the McMenamins Kennedy School is a distinctive hotel. It has a theater, numerous bars and eateries, as well as a spa.

The Society Hotel is a chic, reasonably priced hotel that is situated in Old Town Portland. It features a rooftop deck, individual and communal rooms, and a well-liked cafe.

Made in United States
Troutdale, OR
07/29/2023

11658029R00110